PRAISE FOR
THE SON WILL RISE IN DECEMBER

"How does a young boy find an invincible strength in the midst
of abuse, abandonment, and utter failure of social protection
system in one of the richest countries in the world? How does
anyone survive ruthless hardship time and again and still stay
compassionate for the humankind? Eddie's journey will not
only shake you to the core but also will change your life forever. It is simply an extraordinary book, calling each of us to
rise beyond our limitations and live in the light of our souls'
strength.

—BILLUR SUU, BEST SELLING AUTHOR

"Eddie Pabon has written an extraordinary – and often har-
rowing – narrative of one man's survival. This is a memoire of
an early life filled with loss, cruelty, and hardship, yet Pabon
transcends those dark elements to achieve an existence filled
with hope, love, and forgiveness. Pabon's story is profoundly
moving and – ultimately – an inspiration!"

—WILLIAM E. FOLEY III, PROFESSOR OF PSYCHOLOGY
ADELPHI UNIVERSITY

"In a world of where despair cripple so many, few individuals
are capable of sharing their fears and victories. While reading,
I knew this story needed to be shared with the World. From
darkness to light, this will inspire. I love his grace, love, and
triumph!"

—AMY BROUARD, QMHP, CASAC-T, MSW-I

Claire!

Thank you!

Welcome to my world

Light + Love to you

always

♡

Edward Sloan

THE SON WILL RISE IN DECEMBER

THE SON WILL RISE IN DECEMBER

Eddie Pabon

Printed in the United States of America
First Edition

Cover illustration / Interior Design by Jessie Paulino
Edited by Carissa Bluestone

ISBN 978-0-9991895-3-5

Published by
Voyage to Love Corp,
1392 Madison Avenue, Suite 123,
New York, NY 10029

www.EDDIEPABON.com
Instagram: @HaveHonorHaveFaith
Photography Work: www.LaLecheDelArte.com

DEDICATED

To anyone who has ever suffered at the hands of another.

To all the children who lack true supports.

To the hard workers and underdogs in life.

To those who suffer in silence waiting for their happiness to come.

To anyone who has ever lost someone they truly love.

To my resilient brothers and sisters whom I love more than they will ever understand.

To my mother, Michelle Ramirez, my grandfather, Uncle Lou, Titi Vivian, Uncle Damien, Grandma Selma and all of my loved ones who have passed, may you rest in peace.

And to those who were never there for me.

It's because of you that I found my inner strength.

CONTENTS

FOREWORD

It is impossible to read this book and then forget about it. Because it is impossible that one child, one man, has walked all these miles alone and emerged triumphant.

This is a book of hope. A book that motivates and inspires. Because every challenge that arose was mastered. Every hurdle was overcome. And so begins the journey with the first few steps, the first events that would become a lifetime of hardship. And triumph!

—CAROL ASHLEY, **PHD**

INTRODUCTION

I t **did not take long to** make the decision to immortalize what had happened to me, to all of us. I wanted the struggle to be documented—like Anne Frank's diary—so that others could learn from it. And so that we would never forget...

And so that I would never forget how far I have traveled. You see, across the decades, the edges had blurred. Eddie the caregiver. Eddie the abandoned. Eddie the abused. Eddie the rock! If only I knew then, as I do now, that they were all part of who I am—all part of a larger reality.

The bad and the good synched and made me grow. Like yin and yang. Like the feminine and masculine that are part of two, inseparable wholes. And I was strong! Invincible!

This is my story.

To recreate the events and conversations of this book, I've used my personal memories and journals; the recollections of other family members and family friends who witnessed these events; and print resources, such as articles on my family that appeared in major New York area newspapers as well as documents from the family court system.

I've done my best to piece together a small child's memories and assign dates and locales to those memories whenever possible. That said, it has not been easy to nail down the exact chronology of all the traumatic events my family suffered, especially during the early years of my childhood and the years my siblings and I were shuffled around in the family court system. The stories I chose to include in this volume are the clearest, rawest ones that also feel most important to my journey.

I am blessed to have the support of a few key people in this story. But naturally, others have asked that I maintain their anonymity. I have changed the names and identifying characteristics of some friends and family members to protect their privacy.

PART ONE

EDDIE
THE BOY

"FREDERICK DOUGLASS HOUSES, 1988"

It was twilight. I was in the bath, playing with my toys. I was four.

Suddenly, I heard a scream. It was Mom—she was screaming and crying. Fearfully, I peeked out the bathroom door. My father had a gun in his hand.

"You better open your fucking mouth, bitch!" he screamed.

She begged and pleaded. "Please no! Please stop!"

He put the gun in her mouth and clicked it three times. "This is your fucking lucky day, bitch." Then he pushed her toward the bathroom. I sat on the floor, immobilized, hearing only the sound of my toys dripping on the tile.

The next thing I remember was my mom grabbing me, frantically squeezing me.

She was hysterical. "I love you, papi, I love you . . ."

And this was just the beginning.

1

MOM

How does such a young boy recall his mother's struggles? Well, I saw them, and the images still haunt me. Mom didn't have to tell me her war stories, because I lived through some of her battles.

THE CYCLE BEGINS

My mother's life had always been hard. Mom ran away from home at the tender age of eleven. Her father had beaten her throughout her childhood. He would beat her to a pulp, put her in the hospital, and then continue the beatings there, in the hospital, when she was alone, threatening to kill her if she told anyone. She became a silent victim.

Then she met Dad, the man of her dreams. Or so she

thought. But this relationship quickly turned into a nightmare. The cycle of abuse started by my grandfather (a man I've never met) was continued by my dad.

After years of constantly being approached by pimps and street hustlers, my mom saw a chance for stability with my dad. She was fourteen when they met. He was only fifteen at the time, but he had a good job working for Padded Wagon (a moving company). At first, it was romantic; they fell in love and had babies. I was born in 1984, and my sister Kira was born three years later. But the love story took a sudden twist after that, and the abuse began all over again.

My father used to feed on my mother's fear. Doing the Russian roulette thing. Threatening to shoot her. Laughing at her confusion and fear. He was obsessed with her and with controlling her—Mom would be locked in the apartment so that other men could not even look at her. He beat her daily. When she went out, she wasn't even allowed to look up from the ground when she walked so that she wouldn't accidentally make eye contact with other men.

While we lived at the Frederick Douglass Houses, Dad started selling his Purple Top crack at 105th Street and Columbus. One day, Mom and I decided to call on him there. He was furious. He knocked my mother out stone cold in the middle of the street. He constantly accused her of cheating on him, which was ridiculous because she was held hostage in the apartment all the time. Even outside, Mom remained a hostage. She told me about times when he'd beaten her for no reason or for just for walking outside with her head up. She wasn't allowed to have friends, look out the window, or look at anyone when walking down the street, especially men.

Dad put her through so much. The apartment doors behind which Mom stayed in fear had double-sided locks, and you needed a key to unlock either end. When he came home each day, he would look up at the window, and if he saw her there, he would beat her. There were even times when he'd hit her for looking out the window even though she hadn't been anywhere near it. I have vague memories of some of these beatings.

Mom loved Dad, though. He colored her memories. Made her laugh and cry. Gave her babies. Mom recalled both the good and the bad: their meeting, their struggles, the first blossoms of love. Despite his violent ways, he was charming, and she was smitten.

But eventually, the abuse became too much and Mom left. Dad started having an affair with a woman named Helen and kicked us (Mom, Kira, and me) out of his apartment. We ended up in a domestic violence shelter for a while, and then got an apartment through NYCHA in the projects on the East Side.

THE CYCLE CONTINUES

Sadly, this would not be the last time Mom would suffer at the hands of a man. Shortly after we moved out of Dad's place, Mom got pregnant by her boyfriend Ernie, whom she'd met while he was in jail. Although the abuse had already started long before it, the real shock came after Mom gave birth to my half-sister Callie.

Baby Callie did not stay with us for long. After she had spent a weekend with her father, my mother and her aunt, Titi Ava, noticed swelling and blisters on Callie's private parts while changing her diaper. After an examination in the emergency room, it was concluded that she'd been raped by her father. Mom had met Ernie as a pen pal and had had no idea that he was incarcerated as a convicted rapist. Ernie ran from the police for a few weeks but was eventually caught and arrested. He is still in jail.

My mother's aunt Carla, who had raised Mom, decided to take Callie from Mom and raise her herself. To my mother, this seemed like a betrayal. After all, the family had planned it behind her back. Mom left the baby in the apartment with Carla while she and Titi Ava went to the store. While they were out, Carla removed Callie from our home and went to family court for custody.

It was hard for my mother to process the family betrayal and the loss of her infant daughter. After months of pain and suffering, she moved on, in the face of controversy and Callie's ignorance (even now) about the sexual assault. Callie believes her dad died when she was a baby. Perhaps it is just as well.

The topic depressed Mom and frustrates Titi Ava, who says Mom fabricated the story of the family removing Callie, and that the intervention was necessary considering the facts. Other family members in Florida have a different version of the story—that Mom left the baby alone with many different people many times. I don't recall ever being left with random people, though. Mom was always there for me.

Regardless, why was the same rationale regarding Callie's removal not applied to Kira and me? I'm glad we stayed with Mom, but I always wondered why their intervention was selective.

For Mom there would be so many other betrayals from the system, from a lover. Even life betrayed her!

A FEW GOOD TIMES

We did have some good times in that East Side apartment. Mom threw parties almost every day of the week that were legendary in the projects. People would get drunk and dance, go home to sleep, and be back for more the next day. Crowds were bumping and grinding, the music was thumping, and I would break into dance every now and then. People would stop dancing and point at me and shout, "Look at the little man; he's breaking it down! Go, Eddie! Go, Eddie!"

I needed no invitation. The DJ (his equipment having been stored in my bedroom) kept the beats coming; the crowd was mesmerized by music and drink. If you went into the bathroom to pee, there might be a random couple having sex on the sink. I know. I saw it once.

One time one of Mom's best friends was so drunk she

passed out and everyone got frantic. They carried her into the shower and put her under cold water until she woke up, vomiting. The next night she was back, drinking! The nights were electric!

Then along came Steve . . .

2

STEVE

My story, Mom's story, and Kira's story—all are per-meated by Steve's presence, Steve's influence. Steve was Dad's ex–best friend, and also a crack dealer. I'd find out later that Mom and Steve had started seeing each other while she was still with Dad, though Steve didn't move in with us until we had settled in our East Side apartment after transitioning from the domestic violence shelter. At that point, Steve was doing well as a dealer, and Mom had become obsessed with him.

Steve and Mom had typical ghetto fights all the time. Their on-and-off-again relationship seemed to mirror what Dad and Mom had had—though this time, Kira and I were in just as much danger as Mom.

THE JOURNAL

In elementary school, there was a journal we wrote in every Monday. We wrote about our weekend—our activities and feelings.

I recall one entry went something like this: Dear journal, I had a very bad weekend. Mommy and Steve got into a fight and Steve yelled at her and kicked us out of Albert's house [a friend whose home we lived in briefly]. Mommy cried and Steve took her back.

My teacher asked if I was telling the truth about what I had written. I said yes. At the time I had no concept that my reality was different from other kids' or that the things I had written about were alarming to people, especially coming from a child. My teacher called my mother in when she came to pick me up from school. They discussed my journal entry, and my mother looked at me in surprise.

On our way home she told me that what I had done could've gotten her into trouble. She begged me to never write things like that again.

"But Mom, my teacher wouldn't like for me to write lies. She only accepts the truth of what we did over the weekend as journal stuff," I said. I was so naïve!

My mother looked at me a little sadly because it dawned on her that I was just a child doing an assignment. She said that it was okay to write about the weekend, but I had to avoid bad stuff.

It turned out that Steve had a different view. He became livid and hit me. This was traumatic and humiliating. He said that I "knew what the fuck I was doing," and I'd made him out to be a monster.

Then he said, "You little faggot, go the fuck to your room!"

I was shocked. I had never been reprimanded before, or called a "faggot" for that matter.

I was scared shitless.

I looked at him angrily when he hit me to show him I wasn't

scared. That was the last time I ever thought about making a face. He smacked the crap out of me.

"Don't you ever look at me like that again or I'll fuck you up!" Steve said. Mom had been watching and tried to calm him down.

"I'm tired of this little faggot thinking he is in charge!" he yelled, and he turned on me.

"You are going to start respecting me as your mother's new man or I'm going to start whipping your ass!"

This would be my new hell . . . for a decade.

For the next week after that incident, Mom pleaded with me for forgiveness. She apologized a thousand times. The apologies never stopped coming because every time Steve beat and punished me, Mom apologized. We would wait until he wasn't looking right after he beat me, and we'd give each other what he called "the victim look." Every time I was hit, Mom was feeling the pain with me. Mom wasn't the type to hit, and if she did, she would apologize immediately. Steve hated that and would always say that when I got older, I would hit and disrespect her for not being stern with me from early on.

PRIDE AND JOY

When I was in second grade, my sister Marisa was born, and it was a rare good moment for us.

Marisa was Steve's pride and joy. Of course Kira and I loved her, too. She was our sibling, and a new addition to the family.

But Marisa's presence did not distract Steve from his issues with Kira and me for long. In fact, they grew worse. Steve favored his little girl to the core. We weren't allowed to play with her or do anything that constituted fun. We could feed her, watch her, and change her diapers. This bred resentment toward Marisa, though Kira and I did not plan it. It wasn't until Marisa grew to be about one or two when Steve lost interest with her and started to treat her as one of us.

I recall a time when Marisa was in a walker and learning to

walk. Steve and Mom went to shower. Kira and I had to watch Marisa and stay in our room. Marisa walked over to the door, which was cracked open just slightly. She began to cry, but we calmed her down. Marisa concentrated on the door as Kira and I stood back and observed her. She opened the door progressively, and eventually, she walked through. Kira and I were proud of her and thought Steve and Mom would be excited also.

But of course Steve reacted negatively. "I thought I told you to keep her in the room and watch her!" Our protest was cut off, and he accused us of lying. "Which one of you opened the door and let her out?" Our denial infuriated him.

He didn't or wouldn't believe us. "I'm going to give you both one last chance to tell me the truth before you both get hit."

Needless to say he gave it to us, belt and all, pushing us to admit guilt while he hit us. At first we stood our ground, but after three rounds I lied to make the beatings stop.

He yelled, "I knew it was him! You're a little faggot. You should have been man enough to let me know it was you from the beginning instead of letting your poor little sister get hit for your shit."

As if I had not gone through enough, he hit me three more times and punished me for a week. I was not allowed to talk to or play with Marisa and Kira. I moped around miserably for that week. It seemed that anything I did angered Steve.

THE ENDLESS TUNNEL

And then the nightmares started.

I was running. It seemed like the tunnel was endless. They were always there. Faceless. Merciless. People I did not know. Chasing me . . . Wanting to kill me. And the tunnel went on and on . . . the chase never stopped!

The nightmares haunted me at night. During the day I lived the waking nightmare of Steve's reign of terror.

Imagine . . . I received an excellent report card. Unfortunately, there was a comment about me talking too much during class. This negated the results of my progress. Instead I got a beating!

Steve's punishments were inventive. Sometimes he would make me kneel on grains of uncooked rice while holding the Yellow Pages. It was horrible and humiliating. The rice would roll around under my knees causing excruciating pain. As if this was not enough, if my arms bent or moved at all, he would grab a belt or a phone cord and beat me. Then he'd place me back in the position. I would shake and cry, trying my best to stay still and hold it together, but I wasn't strong enough. He would eventually get mad and grab me, beat me, and tell me what a pussy I was for not being able to handle it. Holding the Yellow Pages exhausted me. At night I would fall asleep instantly, and my body would ache.

The phone cords were the worst because they stung and left marks worse than belts. Those hits hurt like hell, and he didn't swing lightly. Mom always wanted to stop him, but she was helpless to intervene, and did not want to aggravate the situation.

But then there were the telephone cords in the shower. For that, he could get a prize for deliberate and slow torture. Steve would get us butt naked and change the water to a temperature of his choice, usually steaming hot, and beat us with the cord.

I was so scared of Steve that there were times he would leave me alone in the apartment just standing there, facing the wall. He would tell me that if he even felt like I'd moved while they were gone that I would be hit. I kept my ass facing that wall for hours without budging.

Sometimes I almost peed on myself because I had to pee so badly. But I could not risk going to the bathroom in case he returned. He was a miserable asshole. He was a drug addict himself, and he was constantly in a state of withdrawal—which he would, of course, take out on me and Kira.

One of his drug buddies suggested that he use hot sauce in our mouths whenever he felt that we weren't feeling the punishment enough. So then we not only had to face the wall nearly every day but also had to chug spoons of hot sauce. But even this was not enough! This evil man made us hold before swallowing because we needed to feel the burn.

He became even more inventive. Why stop at hot sauce? So he changed it to Jamaican hot sauce to add to the sting. His junkie friends became his advisors on how to punish us.

One time a friend was over at the apartment, and he suggested that Steve put me in the pushup position, because his father used to do that to him and it had worked. So, of course, I was put in the pushup position, which at first I thought would be a breeze. Maybe sixty seconds later I was shaking and struggling to stay in the position.

"You better stay there, you little faggot, or I'll kick you in the stomach," Steve screamed.

And he did just that when I fell the first time. And each time after that for a few minutes. Then I was pushed into the pillows on the bed and told to go to sleep, but to lay face-down in the pillow—just to make sure I didn't become too comfortable. Needless to say no natural movement was allowed, or I would be awakened to a beating for "pretending I was sleeping to try to move."

It seemed like every single day there was a new form of extreme abuse.

THE TORNADO

One day, Kira and I were playing in our room. We had just finished watching a cartoon. The characters were wrapped in a blanket, and the blanket was pulled off. This caused a tornado!

Naturally we wanted to start a tornado too. Kira became the test subject. I wrapped her in a blanket really tight and pulled on the end of it really hard. She spun around and fell to the floor, but on her way down she hit the radiator's solid metal bars. When she stood up there was blood pouring down her face from a head wound.

We panicked. Steve! I begged Kira, "Please shhh."

She tried to stay quiet but was overwhelmed by the sight of so much blood. She began to cry. Steve and Mom ran into the room wanting to know what had happened. I was trying to scoop the blood up back to her head and frantically begged her to be quiet.

"What the fuck is going on here?" Steve shouted.

Mom screamed, "Oh, my god!"

She ran and called an ambulance while Steve yelled some more. "You see, Michelle, this little faggot doesn't even know how to play with his little sister. He did that shit on purpose!" Nothing could stop him.

The ambulance arrived, and Mom went to the emergency room with Kira. Steve grabbed the belt, gave me a few on the head, and made me do one of his favorites: kneeling on rice while holding the Yellow Pages.

I was distraught. Kira came home okay, but she received stitches and she had a bald spot on her head. I got shit from Steve for that bald spot every day while she had it.

THE BANANA PEEL

Another time, I was sick and had these really bad headaches. I was moaning in pain at night, unable to sleep. Steve was annoyed. He yelled at me to shut the fuck up because he was trying to sleep. I tried to be quiet, but the pain was unbearable.

Steve then woke up Mom and instructed her to take me to the hospital before he got mad and beat the shit out of me. I was scared, and Mom told Steve to relax because I was sick. He blew his lid and beat Mom up. He marked her face with a black eye and then kicked us out so he could get some sleep. Mom and I walked to Metropolitan Hospital, crying together. This was the extent of his cruelty and lack of compassion.

When we arrived, the doctors separated us. They wanted

to know what was wrong at home. The doctors tried to question me, but Mom had prepped me on the way. She told me that if anyone asked how she got hurt to say that she fell and hurt herself. One of the doctors closed the door.

"What happened to your mommy's head?" She was really nice.

"She slipped on a banana peel and hurt her eye on a door knob." Despite her persistence, I stuck to my story.

A few minutes later the doctors came in with Mom, and Mom told me I was silly for saying that she'd slipped on a banana peel. That night we returned home and went to sleep. Of course, Steve found a way to blame me, saying I should have been a man and dealt with the pain to have avoided the outcome, thereby saving Mom from being hit for my stupidity.

THE FIRE

Kira also went through hell. I went to school one day, and when I got home, Kira wasn't there. The kitchen and living room were burned, and Mom was stressed out. I asked what had happened, and she explained that Kira had been taken to Bellevue hospital to be evaluated after setting a fire in the house. She was hospitalized for a year.

What I didn't know at the time was that Kira didn't set the apartment on fire intentionally. There had been many times when I was alone in the kitchen and would grab a lighter and set the ants on the window on fire. Kira had been copying me. Unfortunately for her, the curtain caught fire, and the apartment almost burned down. Sadly, as a result of this experience, she had to spend a year in the psych ward for observation. I felt so bad that year and still feel responsible to this day.

DESPERATE MEASURES

It was in this same East Side apartment that I would secretly try to commit suicide. I must have been seven or eight. We were leaving one day, and Steve sent me upstairs to get something he had forgotten. I went into the kitchen and saw them downstairs, walking away to their friend's car, so I knew they wouldn't come inside the apartment. I went into the kitchen drawer and grabbed a knife.

I zipped up my jacket all the way because I thought that my jacket would cushion the pain (I was young). I aimed the knife at my stomach and jabbed it, but it didn't go through the cloth. I tried again, but I could hear Steve screaming from downstairs, "Hurry up, motherfucker!"

I got scared. I was torn between reacting to his anger and wanting to be rid of all this forever. I tried one more time without success, and right before I went to use my full strength, I thought, "What if I succeed in stabbing myself, but I don't die? Then he'll really kill me." So I put the knife away and ran downstairs.

3

HAPPY HOLIDAYS

I learned to approach holidays and special occasions by expecting the worst and hoping for the best. There was no shortage of drama.

HAPPY BIRTHDAY

Not even on my sixth birthday, did I get a break from Steve's wrath. My dad was still dealing drugs and was not around much, but he got me the Super Nintendo (when it first came out) and a 32-inch television for my birthday. I was psyched. I never thought I would get a Super Nintendo and a TV!
The excitement did not last.

Even before Dad brought the gifts by, Steve punished me and forbade me to enjoy my birthday. Steve was a monster, always hungry for his drugs. The little things life brought my way, he ruined. But I had to act cool while Dad walked upstairs. I was so excited Dad had come, and secretly hoped he would save the day.

Every little boy regards their dad as a hero, I guess. I imagined him sensing something was wrong, beating Steve up, and taking me with him. But he didn't. Dad sensed nothing, which to his credit wasn't his fault. I was so scared, I never dared to tell him what was wrong. He asked me why I looked so down on my birthday and why I always had bruises whenever he saw me. How could I respond? I saw Steve in the background. He was watching . . . waiting. Maybe he could lip-read or check out my body language. I could not take that chance.

So I lied and said nothing was wrong and that I was being picked on at school. Strategically my attention shifted to the gifts Dad had brought. All was forgotten. For now. The beatings, the bad vibes . . .

Dad set up the system, and as soon as I began playing, Dad said he needed to get back to business. Predictably, after Dad left I was punished, and Steve played the game. The next day I had school, so I could not play—Steve's rule.

In the morning I was determined to finally be able to play my new game, just like any kid. I was ready for school about a half hour early. I muted the TV. Steve would not notice. Would he?

Channel 3 had black-and-white noise and picture distortion. The volume blasted in the early morning. Quickly, I shut it off. Too late! Steve burst in.

"Didn't I fucking tell you this shit is off limits unless I say you can play?" he yelled. "You don't like to listen, so this is what happens!"

He grabbed the Super Nintendo in one hand and my ear in the other. He dragged me out of the apartment and made me watch him throw the console down the garbage shoot!

I was numb with horror and shock. Then he pushed me into the elevator.

"Go to fucking school, and when you get home, you will be punished."

When I got home, there was no TV. I asked Mom about it. Steve said that it was no longer my TV, and it was in the new apartment we were moving to, waiting for us.

In desperation, I actually believed him. Every day I asked Mom what had happened to the TV, and she maintained that it was waiting in the new apartment. When we actually moved, I asked about it again, and Steve told me that it had broken. I was sad, but it wasn't till years later that Mom and I discussed this. She confirmed that Steve had sold it.

OUR FIRST PET

I love animals, especially dogs. Steve had brought home a pit bull—he was huge and dwarfed me. I loved him dearly until I realized how hard it would be for me to take care of him. Steve would make me walk the dog anyway. He threatened me: If the dog got loose, hurt, or lost, I would be killed. To avoid being killed, I shouldn't even bother to come back home if anything happened to the dog.

So what should have been a happy memory—our beloved dog—became a nightmare, as this big pit bull "walked" me. I was dragged up and down the projects, crying, until someone walking by felt sorry for me and took me back to the building. Many asked why anybody would have me walk this dog. Steve found it all amusing and burst out laughing. He admitted watching me being dragged all over projects through the window for entertainment. Mom eventually made him get rid of the dog because she didn't want me to have to deal with that anymore.

HAPPY THANKSGIVING

One Thanksgiving, we were all enjoying the spirit of the day and everything was great . . . until dinner. Kira had developed an eating disorder. I have many memories of her refusing food and also vomiting incessantly. She didn't like cranberries, so she hesitated when offered them. But of course Steve wouldn't leave her alone.

"You are going to learn to eat and stop your shit. Don't you dare vomit! If you do, I swear you're going to get it." As if she could control it!

She looked scared and nodded for a brief second, then vomited. Steve flipped out. He got up. Tense, we waited.

"You see, she ruined dinner for us! That's why you can´t be nice to these fucking kids!" He reached over, grabbed her by her hair, and marched her to the bathroom. He made her get butt naked and get into the shower while he beat her with a belt. Then he came to get me! He threw me in the shower. With hot water pouring down, he beat me with the phone cord for absolutely no reason.

That was the happy ending to our family's Thanksgiving.

Imagine how Kira, sick, and also three years my junior, must have felt.

(I love you, Kira. Only you and I know what happened to us and nobody else was there for us but Mom. You are a very important person in my life, always. I am proud of the strong woman you have become.)

MERRY CHRISTMAS

Then there was the Christmas when we were celebrating at Selma's (Steve's mother's) house on 92nd Street and Columbus. We had planned a nice Christmas Eve, where we would each open one gift and then go to church. I was so excited.

We are finally going to have a normal Christmas. Or so I thought. At about 10:00 p.m. Steve was becoming frustrated because Selma refused to give him money to go get high before church. She was, after all, the one who had bought all the gifts. And we were about to go to church, she argued. This pissed off

Steve. We could hear him arguing with Mom and Selma.

In the kitchen, Kira and I looked at each other with dread and anxiety. We had gone down this road before! Mom agreed with Selma that Steve should just stay in with the family. As she pleaded, he flipped out and started punching her in the face. I began to cry, and he stopped hitting her and instantly turned and locked eyes with me.

He ran over to me and said, "And you, you little mother-fucker!" He beat me for about a minute until Selma came out of the room frantically screaming, "Here! Please stop, Steve. Please calm down and take the money!"

She had twenty dollars in her hand. She begged him to take it and go get high. Steve needed no invitation. He took the money and stormed out of the apartment to go get his fix. Mom, as always, came over to me and hugged me, crying and apologizing for what he had just done. We cried together and wound up staying home that night.

That was our merry Christmas Eve. Another disastrous holiday! The next day we opened our gifts as if nothing had happened. That was life for us. One minute good, then very, very bad.

4

RECIPE FOR DISASTER

Mom **always looked for ways** to have an open line of communication. She suggested many times, in many different forums, that family talks should take place. I remember countless pleas from her to Steve to consider healthier approaches to discipline.

Needless to say, it never worked because Steve couldn't handle us stepping out of a child's place and expressing negative feedback. I overheard a conversation in which Mom suggested that Steve ask Kira and me to draw a picture of what we thought of him. She said she had seen it on a TV show and thought it was a good idea.

This was a recipe for disaster. Despite his agreement, I felt scared.

He reassured us that we could open up and come clean

about how we felt about him. He was warm and in a great mood. He hugged us and told us how much he loved us—more than "that faggot sperm donor we called our father." We started drawing.

Kira drew Steve holding a belt and standing with all of us: Kira, Marisa, and me. It showed Steve and Mom holding hands, and there were stars, birds, grass, and a big sun in the top corner. I, on the other hand, drew him as a devil, with horns and a tail, beating me with his trident staff while he yelled and I cried. Hey, I was being honest.

Steve preferred that Kira start, because he knew that she loved him and that I didn't like him at all. He sensed I would portray him to be a monster.

They laughed at her drawing. It amused them: a happy family holding hands, with stars, birds . . . and Steve with a belt.

Now I was scared. It seemed that Kira and I had drawn exactly what Steve expected we would.

I hesitated to show them my drawing, and Steve said that if I didn't want to present it, I didn't have to, so I chose not to. But Mom insisted. She said that she wanted me to start talking about my feelings. I was reassured that this was a safe opportunity to express myself. Hesitantly, I showed them the picture.

Everything froze. All was silent.

"Is this how you feel?" Mom was concerned.

I responded nervously, "Yeah."

Steve responded as I had dreaded.

"I knew he was going to do this, this fucking kid. He always has to make me out to be the devil."

Steve fucked me up and sent me to my room. He and Mom got into a fight because Mom was pissed that he'd hit me when I was just opening up. After all, they had assured me I could. Steve argued that those weren't my feelings. I was just drawing that to be spiteful.

As a child, I would never express my feelings about Steve

in any way again.

That had to wait till my adulthood.

5

GETTING BY

We were so poor, it was ridiculous. But somehow we made it through.

Things like soap for a bath were scarce at times, and we had to use dishwashing liquid or laundry detergent. When there was no money to wash clothes, which was often, we washed them by hand. We would fill up a bathtub and separate the clothing into whites and colors. Then we would either pour detergent, dishwashing liquid, or body soap onto the clothing and use the scrub brush that's supposed to be used for cleaning the bathtub. After we scrubbed them till our muscles hurt, we would leave them soaking and move onto the next article of clothing. When everything was scrubbed, Kira and I would take turns stomping on the clothes to try to simulate what a washing machine did. Then we would empty the bathtub and squeeze the clothes dry.

For big stuff like jeans, Mom and I would grab one end each and twist it into opposite directions as far as we could. Then we would hang the clothing out to dry. Sometimes the clothes took a day to dry, sometimes two. Steve never washed clothes with us.

We didn't mind doing the wash by hand, because that was how we were accustomed to doing it. It was habitual: when you took off your socks, you went and scrubbed them in the sink or tub and hung them to dry. Sometimes this method backfired—the clothing wouldn't dry fast enough and would begin to smell. I hated this because it created an opportunity for my schoolmates to ridicule me.

SCHEMES AND SCAMS

Steve and Mom found schemes to get by with everything. For example, we would never pay any phone or cable bills. We would let them rise to as much as we could and call the cable company or phone company to ask for extensions, until there were no more options and the services were cut off. Then Mom would call a new company and switch and repeat the process. When all companies were used, Mom would use another one of our social security numbers to start the process all over under a different name. (Of course, this backfired on me when I became of age and discovered what credit was. My report showed I owed thousands of dollars to phone and cable companies.)

They even got cigarettes and baby products for free. Mom would write to Newport and say that she had bought two cartons of cigarettes that were all stale. She would say that when she attempted to return the cigarettes, the supermarket or store wouldn't exchange or refund them because the cartons had been opened. Within two weeks a response letter would arrive from Newport apologizing and notifying her that within another week or so she would receive two free replacement cartons.

This strategy was repeated with Johnson & Johnson baby bottles and products. She would write to them saying that there was a hole in the bottle she purchased or she or the baby got burned because the plastic melted, and she would receive coupons for free bottles, etcetera.

One time when we lived with Pops (Steve's dad), we received catalogs to sell candy for fundraising, as was the annual practice at all public schools. Steve made Kira and me go to buildings on West End Avenue where rich folk lived to try to sell to them. The only problem was that whenever we received cash for payment, Steve would take it. This became one of Steve's short-term hustles. We never actually got to sell the candy. We would knock door to door selling candies and make hundreds of dollars in sales and never get to earn a prize at school for our work. I hated it because there were cool prizes that I could have earned if Steve hadn't taken the money.

EDDIE THE BREADWINNER

I always tried to make money to help my mother. Even as a child of about seven, I would ask her permission to go and "play" with my friends outside. Then I would walk outside the projects without her knowing. I'd dig in garbage cans and take out the aluminum cans, go to the supermarket, and cash them in for a refund. I would bring the money home (small amounts), and she would always ask me, "Papi, how did you get this money, and how come every time you go outside you come back with change or money?"

"I just got it, Mommy . . . I found it." I would reply.

One day a friend of my mother's saw me digging in the garbage on 106th Street. I got scared when she questioned me and said nothing.

"Don't dig in the garbage . . . that's dirty and nasty."

I nodded and said okay, waited till she left, and continued

on as before. She told Mom immediately.

Mom waited for me to get home and said, "Papi, you don't need to do that. I love you for thinking about helping Mommy, but don't do that anymore."

I don't think I ever did again. Instead I went to the supermarket (Pioneers on 106th and 1st) where I always cashed in the cans and spoke to the manager, who allowed me to become a bag packer. I packed bags there every day instead of playing with the kids outside.

Making money to help Mom was fun to me because the little ounce of praise I received always made me feel needed and important. I practically raised the kids. All of their first words were my name.

Packing bags brought in quite a bit of money—it really helped us through bad times.

When my little brother Robert was born, our financial instability worsened. On Robert's first birthday, I went and packed bags as usual, but this time I had a secret plan for the money I earned. I purchased teething toys, brand-new bottles, Pampers, a pacifier, a cake, and a number one candle for him.

After all, it was his birthday. Mom was taken aback. I could see that she was disappointed because I used all the money for Robert's birthday instead of for food. But, being Mom, she respected what I did and thanked me for being a good brother. I could see that she was proud of me. She knew that I loved my brother. She hugged me and said, "I don't know what I would do without you."

6

QUESTIONING

As though there wasn't enough on my plate just dealing with the violence around me, I also started questioning my sexual identity at a young age.

I clearly remember my first sexual experience, which happened when I was a very small child. It was during kindergarten. I had a classmate who was my "bathroom buddy." Anthony and I would go to the bathroom several times during the school day, till the teacher stopped the many bathroom visits. We touched each other in the stalls. It was pretty innocent and childish stuff, but we both liked it.

Eventually, we were caught and ridiculed by other kids. We ran back to class when they threatened to tell the teachers on us.

And then they did what kids do and almost in sync, said,

"Ewww. He's a boy touching another boy's pee-pee. Ewww."

I tried to tell Mom about me being gay. No one was interested in hanging out with me, so I was a bit of a loner. Some were too young, and older kids thought I was too young. But I knew I was different.

Mom was watching her soap operas, as she did every day like clockwork (One Life to Live, All My Children, and General Hospital). I heard one of the characters "coming out of the closet" to his parents, telling them he was gay. I asked, "Mom, what's gay?"

"Gay is when boys like boys, papi, or girls like girls."

I thought for a second, and it hit me that that's what was different about me.

"Don't worry, papi. You're not gay, so it doesn't apply to you."

"Yes, I am, Mommy. I am gay."

"Don't be silly, spaghetti Eddie. You're not gay, papi—you don't understand what gay really is."

I began to get a little scared about pressing the issue, so I left it alone and went about playing with my toys. All I could think of that day was that I was not normal. I had to be quiet. I had to avoid getting into trouble. I could feel that this was a taboo subject. Liking boys was something I started to think about a lot.

ANDREW

When I was still in elementary school, and we were living temporarily in one of Pops' apartments in Ozone Park, Queens, we met a man named Andrew. He must've been in his thirties (at least). He was a white guy who first befriended Steve and would soon after became someone I'd never forget.

I can't provide too many details as to what the true nature of Andrew's relationship with Mom and Steve was, because I honestly don't know. What I do remember was that I liked Andrew and he knew that. I would be playing with my toys outside, and he'd walk up to me, smile, and say hello. Shyly, I'd respond.

We played football or baseball. He offered many times to take me to Mets games at Shea Stadium. When the subject of Andrew's girlfriend came up, Andrew would say that they were on bad terms and hadn't spoken for a while. He lived alone in a room in lower Manhattan.

Eventually, I accompanied him to a baseball game. It was fun, different from the norm at home, and a break from the abuse. I remember on the way back home, Andrew put his hand on my lap and rubbed it. I had no concept of what a pedophile was or that this behavior was not normal. I took it as affection, and to be really honest, I liked it. It turned me on in some naive and clueless way. I let him touch me. While he did, he asked if I liked the baseball game, and if I liked him touching me like that. Yes, and yes . . . someone was being nice to me. What was not to like? He grabbed my hand and put it on his hard penis. I was both a little scared and excited.

There were many more baseball games. Mom and Steve started to become curious as to the true nature of this relationship. There were many questions. Did he touch you? Don´t worry, you won't get into trouble.

Yeah, right! I thought. My honesty had earned me only punches and beatings before. So I denied it.

After a few months, we went to another Mets game. After the game Andrew said he had to pick something up at home before dropping me off. He said he had a Nintendo that I could play and he would have me back in no time. I was super excited about being able to play the Nintendo, and Mom and Steve had agreed to let me go before being dropped off.

This time the touching was frantic. Again, I can't lie, I liked it. When we got to his apartment, he put on the video game and proceeded to remove his clothing as any normal person would do (or so I thought). He eventually stripped down to his boxers at which point I noticed his penis. I said I wanted to watch TV after I got bored with the game, and Andrew walked over to the TV, turned off the game system, and put in a video cassette. The video he put in was porn of some white women having hardcore sex. I was nervous and embarrassed because I hadn't been exposed to porn yet and this was new for me.

Andrew sat me on his lap where I felt his penis rubbing on my butt. I got off his lap and grabbed it with my hands. He asked me to put it in my mouth, but it didn't fit. He jerked it off in my face for about two minutes until the phone rang. He got up to answer, and to his disappointment, it was Mom. She demanded he bring me back to Pops' house immediately. He was frustrated and went off about how they shouldn't have let me come over and then waited so late to have him bring me back. He drove me home, and after he left, Mom and Steve grilled me. Did he touch you? If so, did it feel normal?

Of course I lied. I'd be hit if I told the truth.

But I guess Mom was really in tune with what was going on. She was Mom. She had instincts. And it didn't sit right with her.

So that was the end of Andrew. I never heard from him again. To this day I wonder what would've happened to me if Mom hadn't called that night.

Regardless, the seed had been sown. I was curious about my sexuality. This curiosity grew with every moment that passed.

7

KINGPIN

As the years went by, Dad rose from dealer to king-pin, the head man in charge of a major drug ring. As far back as I can remember, drugs were a big part of my life. Dad was part of the Purple Top crew and was head in a chain of command of over fifty dealers. Kira and I would sit and separate Dad's money (ones, fives, tens, and twenties), and we would steal a five-dollar bill every now and then to bring home to Steve and Mom.

Dad's friends (the dealers) would be sitting at the table cutting the crack while he cooked it in his apartment. He used a coffee pot and would watch it heat carefully. My father was respected everywhere we went. He always had new cars and women. From the time I was a kid till this day I have always loved him and looked for his attention and approval.

Unfortunately, in those early years, I would learn that my father's love didn't extend beyond dumping us on someone else. He only knew how to pacify us with money until the weekend was over.

While we valued the time with him, he obviously did not feel the same. Still I had faith in my father and loved him anyway, and I was devastated when, eventually, in 1994, he went to jail for drug trafficking.

And even though he was part of the cycle of violence in our family, I never held any hard feelings against my dad for what he did to my mother—at least not as a child. I can remember that on every New Year's, Christmas, birthday, etcetera, I would beg to see my dad. Steve hated it and forbade Mom from letting us go to see him. When I cried for my dad, Steve would say that I was crying for attention and to make Mom feel bad. This, of course, wasn't my intention, but I stopped crying about him because Mom would look at me with a sad face like she felt my pain—and any mention of Dad angered Steve.

THE PIZZA SHOP

When I was a little boy, Dad would take me to his drug block and leave me in the pizza shop on 105th and Columbus. He would give me what felt like countless change and leave me playing arcade games while he handled his business. I loved it!

I actually got into my first fight in that pizza shop. I was playing Mortal Kombat (at the time, the newest arcade), and an older and bigger kid came and told me he would play the game for me. He tried to push me out of the way. I repeatedly said no, and when he threatened to hit me, I lost it and we fought for a few seconds. The manager of the pizza shop broke up the fight. I felt like the man that day because when Dad came back to pick me up, the pizza shop manager told him about the fight. Dad was so proud of me. He boasted to all of his friends about it. He even celebrated a little momentarily. He requested that the manager blast a song on the radio so I could dance. Then the chanting began, "Go, Eddie! Go, Eddie!"

He did that often, getting me to break into dance to impress his friends. I always burst into doing the running man and winding.

There was this other time that Dad picked me up for the weekend and dropped me off at his neighbor Stan's for the day. He gave Stan $500 and asked that he go and pay his Motorola beeper bill for him and then use the rest of the money to take me out for fun. Stan and I went and paid the bill, which was about $250.

Then Stan took me to eat, which still left him with a nice chunk of money. We agreed to go play arcades with the money in the local pizza shop while we waited for Dad to pick me up. I had a blast that day. Stan had given me at least $50 in quarters to play arcades. We had a crowd around us watching us play game after game for hours. Those had been good times!

JOANNA AND HELEN

My dad hit me only one time that I can remember and it paled in comparison to what I was used to with Steve. Dad was too busy dealing with his business to have time to beat up his kids. However, I do remember the countless times he beat his girlfriends, Joanna and Helen.

Joanna I remember more clearly, because 90 percent of the time Dad would take us to her house. She had more privileges than Mom but endured the same domestic violence. For example, she could go outside and take me to the park in front of the building on 100th Street. But Dad would come home randomly and beat her, then leave (at least that's what I observed). After he'd leave, Joanna would cry and I would go to her, hug her, and apologize. She would ask me to ask my dad to please stop hitting her. I realized the wisdom of not doing that: She would be beaten again.

Helen used to get it pretty bad. I had gone with her to the store once and the cashier told her to have a nice day. She replied politely. At home when Dad asked if she had spoken to anyone, I burst out like an idiot and said, "Oh yes, she did!" I swear I didn't think she would be beaten up. I was one of those kids who didn't grasp the concept of consequences. So I gave a blow by blow account of the cashier and poor Helen.

"Yes, it was a guy, and he said have a nice day, and she said thanks, you too." Helen defended herself and said it was just a guy at the store behind the register. Dad flipped out and beat her. He punched her in the face a few times and pushed her into the room, where the screams, bangs, and pleading continued.

I remember being at Helen's apartment and Dad coming in with a tan. Helen asked him what he was doing, and if he had gone to the beach with "some bitches." He threatened to hit her and swore that he had been on the roof having a few drinks with some friends. A few minutes later Helen left to go to the store, and while she was gone, I overheard Dad on the phone talking to his friend.

"Yeah, man, this bitch keeps asking me what we were doing, so if she asks, just tell her we were on the roof. Yeah, man, that bitch I met at the beach was bad, right? Anyways, let me let you go because she's coming up the block now."

I felt bad for Helen, and I had it set that when she came home, I would tell her. I felt like that would make up for getting Helen hit after I told Dad about the cashier. I thought it wasn't fair to her that she couldn't lie to him, but he had lied to her.

So while he was in the shower, I whispered to her that he lied and told her about how he had met women on the beach. Helen was enraged and approached him right away.

I was shocked.

Dad ran out of the bathroom and began yelling at me, saying that I was the one lying. One thing led to another, and when I innocently pointed out that he was the one lying, he punched me in the face. I fell on the floor next to the table in the kitchen. I moved under it. He tried to get me out, while cursing and shouting.

"How fucking dare you, little snitch! You're supposed to have my back. You don't turn on me for no bitch!"

Then he beat Helen and left. When he was gone, Helen approached me in tears and apologized to me for saying anything. She then thanked me for being honest. That was the first time Dad ever hit me. I'll never forget that because it was also the last time.

KIRAS TURN

That wasn't the first time that one of us (Kira or I) had accidentally told Helen about one of Dad's girlfriends. Dad always had strange women taking care of us. Usually when one woman left, a few minutes later the next would enter. This was the norm for us. So being children, we would slip up every now and then and say things we weren't supposed to. Well, this incident occurred while Dad was with Helen but cheating with Joanna. At the time Helen lived in the Brooklyn/Queens border area, and Joanna lived one building down from Dad's apartment. Helen was in the apartment making us lunch as usual and getting ready to leave. I overheard Helen asking Kira, "Does your dad ever have other girls here?"

"Mmm-hmm." Kira was just being honest. Helen knew she had stumbled onto something, so she started digging for more.

Kira went shooting off at the mouth about everything. "The girl's name is Joanna, and she lives next door in the other building. She cooks for us just like you, and she comes here every time you leave."

A few hours later, Dad returned, and innocently, I quietly told him what happened. He went straight to the kitchen and acted like everything was cool, until Helen blurted out the question.

"So you have other women here taking care of your kids when I am not around?"

"Do me a fucking favor and don't EVER question my kids

about me, bitch! Are you fucking crazy asking them those questions?" He was beating her while he ranted. Then I saw him grab Kira, hit her, and toss her into the bedroom while yelling, "You never snitch on me, bitch. I am your fucking father!"

I can't recall Helen ever asking us questions again after that incident.

So from one year to the other, somehow, we were surrounded by violence.

8

WITNESS PROTECTION

While my dad had become a kingpin, Steve, too, had risen the ranks. During the end of our stay in the East Side apartment, Steve had become a big-time drug dealer. He had friends who were connected to major suppliers. For example, there was my father's connection, "Caboz," who supplied kingpins like my father. Then there was "Little Willie," a drug dealer and friend of Steve's.

Steve and Little Willie had several meetings in the apartment. One discussion was about robbing someone huge—when the apartment would be guarded, the best time to hit, what guns to bring, and contingency plans if caught. I didn't understand the severity of whom they were planning to rob until later in life.

When the day of the robbery arrived, Mom was nervously

pacing back and forth for hours, waiting ... Eventually, Steve came back, agitated and breathless. They had robbed the apartment at the wrong time—and then Little Willie had to take a shit. So they got caught! There was an exchange of gunfire. They'd gotten away with a few kilos of coke, but they thought they may have been recognized.

A couple of nights later the sound of two gunshots at the apartment door shattered the calm. Mom screamed. Steve made us hit the floor. I was scared. Mom was frantic. I started crying. "Shut up!" Steve yelled as he ran to the safe to get his gun.

The banging on the front door did not stop. Steve shot back. All became quiet. Mom called the cops. "Oh, my God. Oh, my God. They're trying to kill us!" she told the operator. Mom and Steve were frantic. The cops arrived, and some detectives escorted us to a Days Inn motel after questioning Mom and Steve.

Under witness protection we were moved around to all kinds of hotels in several states in the Northeast. We spent six months hopping from Holiday Inns to Days Inns, and any other motel they could find. But they couldn't keep us safe.

We would be traced to a motel by the (prospective)killers, and the police would rush us to a new state or apartment temporarily, paid for by the program. A few placements later, new detectives were assigned to our case. When we met with them at 100 Centre Street in Lower Manhattan, they explained that we were being moved constantly because the bad guys had intel as to where we were being placed.

After that we were rushed onto a plane and given a home in California without further explanation. After the move we learned that one of the district attorneys originally assigned to our case was dirty, which is why we had been moved out of the tristate area. The story even made the Daily News!

The dirty DA had been a cousin of my father's contact, Caboz. Steve was helping the police to put Caboz away in exchange for protection, and it was he who had a hit out on us.

According to Steve, my father knew all about it! This life we led, this story, had the makings of a James Bond movie.

I remember asking my dad years later what he had done to protect us and why he didn't fight Caboz. Dad said that he did approach Caboz and asked that he spare Kira and me. He said that he paid Caboz $10,000 for us to be spared.

But I was still mad at him! It seemed like he had been stupid—the first kid the hitmen would've tried to kill would've been me. After all, I was the oldest and could point them out in a line up.

How could I get over that?

CALIFORNIA

The house in California was amazing. It was in Palm Springs, out in the desert. The nearest store was miles away. I loved it and so did Mom.

But to Steve it meant:

1. He needed to get a job to pay the rent on the house because the DA's office wasn't going to pay for it except for the down payment.

2. He didn't have access to drugs like he did in New York.

I was registered for school, and we eventually became acquainted with our neighbors. This was the most normal living experience we'd had. Mom loved the public assistance rate for food stamps and the cash and rent assistance she was receiving. I know because she boasted about the differences between California and New York regularly.

We all had our own rooms. I even had my own bathroom access from my bedroom! Our neighbors were great people with heavy country accents. I made some friends for a change and loved the school system. It was in the middle of the desert, and the activities we did in class were nothing like the usual New York school activities. Instead of big, overcrowded buildings with hustle and bustle, there we were in a quiet desert, with huts as classrooms and significantly smaller class sizes. This meant more attention and a more personal experience. My favorite things about living in California were catching lizards in the backyard, the way it rained in the desert (heavily, randomly, and fast, which was beautiful and fun), and the coyotes that came out into the backyard and howled. They would even scratch at the windows. Fearfully, I would look out of my window and watch packs of coyotes.

But sadly, within two months of living there, the bills began to pile up. The electricity and rent were overdue, and the water was about to get cut off. All in all, things weren't looking good. Steve decided to leave us in California to go back to New York to sell drugs and make money for us. Mom didn't like the idea but had no choice but to let him go.

About a week after Steve left, Mom went to the neighbors' house to call Pops, Steve's father. She learned that Steve had been arrested. Pops arranged to send her money through Western Union, and the neighbors gave her some extra money; it was enough for plane tickets to New York for all of us.

MIDDLETOWN

And so we left the beauty and quietude of California behind. We bailed Steve out of jail. We stayed at Pops' house, and about a month later, Caboz was finally arrested. After that, Steve was rewarded with a house in Middletown, New York, and was paid $5,000 for his part in the arrest. Initially, things were looking up. Steve was much happier and so I got into trouble less often. He was so caught up in the payday he'd received that nothing else mattered.

Once again we were given a beautiful house and furniture. It also meant moving schools once again, this time to Truman Moon Elementary School.

The DA's office had covered the down payment on the house and furnished it, but the monthly expenses and bills were left to Mom and Steve.

The pending monthly bills were obviously a disaster waiting to happen all over again. As young as I was, I realized that Steve and Mom weren't experienced enough to have a house or financially capable of sustaining it. One would think that the DA would've learned from the last experience!

The gas was soon shut off for not being paid and the electricity was often off as well. Steve would always say he was going to the city to get money when he was really abandoning ship and going to get high. Mom and I would ask neighbors for food until their goodwill was exhausted. I tried looking for work. I advertised on signs that I would clean people's houses, but that didn't happen. We were starving and had no phone or TV, so I resorted to walking miles to the nearest store to try to sell my comics. Collecting Marvel comic books and cards was the craze back then, and I accumulated a pretty decent collection for a poor kid.

After walking for miles—yes, miles—I got to the comic store and tried to sell my stuff. The store assistant seemed annoyed and told me the buyer wouldn't be in for a couple of hours. I walked the miles back and told Mom. She cried, hugging and thanking me and telling me that she loved me. She said that I didn't have to keep going to the store because it was really far and she was concerned for my safety. I told her I was going anyway, and a few hours later, I walked there again with my comics in hand. When I got back to the store, the guy who bought comic books and cards laughed. "Get out of here, kid. Those things are worthless."

I had made two long trips for nothing! Sadly, I trudged back home. I wasn't mad about the walk or anything other than the fact that I couldn't rescue Mom and she would still be stressed out. When I got home I was exhausted. Mom hugged me and thanked me for trying. As I looked at her I could see that this reality was concerning her more and more. I went to play at a neighbor's house, and luckily, they were eating dinner. They offered me food and I took it, ate a little, and asked to take the rest to Mom and the kids.

After a few days, Steve showed up with a stolen station wagon and some money for food. We all got into the station wagon and drove to the nearest grocery store.

On our way to the store, we were pulled over and Steve was asked for his license and registration. Steve lied and said he forgot his wallet with the license. The officers went back to their car and ran the plates. Meanwhile, Steve considered speeding off.

"Fuck, Michelle. They are going to arrest me! Should I drive off?" he asked Mom.

"No, Steve, don't!"

He looked in the mirror repeatedly until the cops returned. He was pulled out of the car and cuffed. The cops asked us to get out of the vehicle and walk home. Mom pleaded with the officers to help us get home because we had no other means to get us there. The officers were rude. It wasn't their issue, they said. So Mom, Kira, Marisa, Robert, and I walked to the nearest exit and found a local shopping area.

Mom begged for a quarter as people walked by, and she got one and used it to call Pops. I began playing with a little boy, showing him my Marvel cards. He liked a card I had in my hand, and I offered it to him to keep. After all, they were worthless to me after that guy rained on my reality. The kid ran to his mother and told her that I'd given him the card. She then walked over to Mom, who was crying on the phone, and tried to thank her for my kindness. When Mom finished her phone call, the woman asked, "What's wrong? Is everything okay? I am sorry for being nosey but was trying to thank you for your son's kindness. He gave my son a card, and I thought that was sweet."

Mom explained the situation, and the lady offered to drive us back home. As we headed home, Mom looked at me and said, "I love you, papi. You're my guardian angel from God, here to help me without even trying sometimes."

I smiled, and the woman agreed that I was special. I was happy—I had saved the day once again. When we got home, we waited there until Pops came and picked us up to take us back to his apartment. Mom gathered all our belongings and abandoned our new house to go to back to the city.

9

THE
PUPPY

When we were back in the city, I had one of the worst birthdays I can recall. I must have been nine or ten. Steve and Mom came home with a new puppy for me. I instantly loved this puppy and spent the next few hours petting and admiring it. She was small, all white, and the best birthday present I'd ever been given (other than the Nintendo and TV my dad had tried to give me at age six).

We had been over at 100th and Columbus, where my mom's friend Miranda and my aunt Ava lived, when the dog was given to me. I played outside, showing off my new dog. After a few hours had passed, Steve started to become annoyed with me being so excited with the new dog and reminded me of the fact that we were staying in someone's house where the dog wasn't welcome. (At the time we'd been crashing with some friends of

Mom and Steve's a few blocks away.)

The message was clear: the dog would not be mine for long. As we walked I became depressed. I couldn't understand why he would give me a dog just to take it away from me.

Of course I understand now that it was part of the manipulation, the twisted way in which he reasoned!

Mom came around and tried to make me feel better. She reassured me that she would do everything in her power to make sure the dog would remain in my arms. Then we bumped into a crackhead named Eric who walked up to me and tried to grab the dog.

"Yo, what the fuck are you doing?" said Steve.

Eric apologized to Steve and explained that the dog wasn't his to sell in the first place. He needed to return the dog to its owner because they threatened to call the police on him. Steve flipped.

"Are you fucking crazy, bro?"

Eric apologized again, and Steve pulled out a box cutter. Eric began to plead and beg Steve for forgiveness, and Mom began screaming, "Please, Steve, calm down. Let's just go."

Steve told her to shut the fuck up, and the look on his face changed as he approached Eric, who was trying to get away. Steve's look was like an evil grin. He began swinging the blade at Eric, and all I could see was Eric starting to bleed from his face, then his entire body.

"Please stop! Steve, stop!" Mom was screaming. Eric was begging for Steve to stop. There was blood everywhere! Steve must have cut that poor man at least ten times all over his face and arms. (Eric kept covering his face with his arms.) Steve yelled at us to shut the fuck up and run with him.

Eric fled in the opposite direction. As we ran Steve stopped really quickly and disposed of the blade in a garbage can, took off his shirt because it had blood on it, and instructed us to calm down. He was in control, smoothly, quickly, as if it had never happened.

Mom was crying. We were crying. It was a mess. When we

got home, I held on to that dog like I was its only hope. Steve noticed that I hadn't said anything, and that I was clinging to the dog. He yelled, "You see what the fuck happened because of you, you little faggot. I had to fight for that fucking dog. Give me that dog."

He took the dog and brought it downstairs to the car that belonged to the people who we were staying with at the time. When he left Mom looked at me and told me it wasn't my fault.

"At least you got to keep the dog."

I spent that night so depressed, because even though I knew the dog was in the car, I felt like it was a matter of time before Steve took it from me. A hollow victory. He knew it made me happy, so he had to take it away—just as he took away every vestige of hope, of happiness, I had ever known.

Needless to say, there was no dog in the car next day.

Instead there was a note that read: We took the dog from the car because it's cruel to leave an animal hungry and crying alone in a car all night. If you call the police we will report you for animal cruelty in our defense. The dog has a new home now where it will be taken care of.

I cried so much that day. Mom kept trying to make me feel better about it and was just as hurt as I was.

A little over a month later, Mom and I were walking down the street, and we saw a Caucasian woman with two dogs. One of them immediately caught my eye because it was smaller and it was completely white just like mine. I got really excited and said, "Mom look, look . . . the dog."

Mom said, "Oh shit, Eddie, that is the dog."

As we approached the lady, she noticed we were coming and asked if we were the people who left the dog alone. We said yes, and before we could say anything else, the woman said, "Well, she has a new owner now, and she's more than taken care of. I'm sorry for taking the dog, but she was in the car, screaming and starved, and leaving her there was just wrong."

"But it wasn't in your place to take my son's dog!"

The Son Will Rise In December   51

cried Mom.

"Well, I'll call the police because I've had her for almost a month, have taken good care of her, and she is mine now."

I hugged the dog, and Mom and I let it go.

I had to leave the moment, as I had to leave behind so many moments.

As we walked away, I began to cry, and Mom comforted me. "The dog is with someone who could love, feed, and house it," she said. "Let it go, papi."

So I did. But I didn't feel any better.

10

THE CHELSEA PROJECTS

While we were staying with Pops, Mom registered me for sixth grade at Lincoln Academy. Kira was also there, in the elementary school.

THE GOOD SAMARITAN

Kira had been placed into special education classes because she'd had difficulty learning to read and write. She also attended an after-school reading program where there was a volunteer who would soon become not only a long-term mentor but also a mother figure to her. Her name was Diane Sawyer. She was interested in Kira's education—and soon after, in her personal life too. Diane saw a little girl with potential but a poor support system. So she took Kira on recreational outings, including trips to her ranch to ride horses. Diane always made sure to send Kira a gift for Christmas and kept in contact.

Needless to say, it was not long before Steve and Mom found this to be an opportunity for more than support for Kira. Diane assisted Mom in obtaining housing in the projects in Chelsea. We secured a large, three-bedroom apartment that accommodated our entire family. Mom was grateful and Steve wanted to get anything out of Diane he could think of. He would make Kira contact Diane's assistant and ask for money for supposed school supplies and food. Diane, of course, would immediately cut a check for Kira for her needs.

One time she sent a limousine to the apartment to deliver catered food. Kira hated this because she appreciated the natural support and love she received from Diane and did not want to lose her or make her think that she was just using her for her money. (Fortunately for Kira and me, Diane maintained her love and support over the years, seeing us for who we are as individuals. She is more than a mentor; she is family. For that I am grateful.)

THE PROFESSIONAL INFORMANT

Even after we moved into the Chelsea projects, Steve continued to work for the DA. By this time, because he had helped them get Caboz, he had the power to have people arrested—and make money from it! After Caboz, he went for my dad! Then he went for more members of the Purple Top crew. Steve had become "arrest and get paid" crazy! No one was safe.

I remember sitting in the room downtown at 100 Centre Street, where they would play videotapes of my dad and other people who worked for him on the block. They had cameras on the rooftops and streetlights, along with wiretaps and recordings of all their moves. Steve would point people out and explain who they were and what position they were in, where they lived, and who they were related to. Sometimes they would ask me about these suspects. I would play dumb and plead ignorance. I had to protect Dad! How I longed to tell him of Steve's snitching, his evil plans.

But I couldn´t. I was paralyzed by my fear of the consequences. Steve didn´t play around. After all the arrests, including Dad's, the DA began to notice that Steve was just as dirty as everyone they had convicted. He had made the mistake of getting arrested one too many times to the point where knowing the DA and working for them wasn't holding weight in court anymore. He began to make plea bargains, agreeing to help them make a certain number of arrests, this time in exchange for his freedom. Steve knew he couldn't follow up those arrests because half the people he was promising to help catch didn't even exist.

So after being released from his last arrest, he went on the run. He had exhausted his usefulness and the DA's goodwill. The DA would constantly call at Pops' apartment and look for him, but we pretended that he was out on business with these imaginary people. For example, he had lied and said that he was on to some big-time mafia connection that he was going to help the DA bring down. They didn't believe him, but he swore that he was legitimate. He was literally just lying around the apartment and going about his business getting high all day. Whenever the DA called, Mom would say she hadn't seen Steve for weeks and that he was undercover with these mafia men who would kill him if he had any contact outside of them. The DA knew he was full of shit but played along until they got tired and put a warrant out for his arrest.

A TURN FOR THE WORSE

So many things happened in a short time after we moved into the Chelsea projects. While Steve was dodging the DA, Mom gave birth to Sara and become pregnant with Tamara.

Having more mouths to feed worsened our precarious financial situation. In addition, Steve and Mom were seriously strung out on heroin. We were always hungry and never had enough money for anything because all food stamps and public assistance were cashed by Steve. He did this routinely so he could buy his heroin. As a result we had exhausted all other options in asking neighbors, family, and friends for food. So we resorted to stealing from supermarkets. Steve had noticed that we kids could successfully steal on a regular basis, so he became creative. Why not use us and our new "gift" to steal from the shopping centers on 34th Street. He could sell the proceeds, not for food, but for him, the ever innovative Steve. Kira and I were instructed to go to Kmart, Conway's, Woolworths, and Macy's to steal things like batteries and cameras that he could resell to stores on 125th Street. Places like Conway's provided opportunities to get clothing for us kids. The first time we tried, we successfully stole a camera or two, a few 4-packs of double-A batteries and one or two shirts from Conway's. This was awesome to Steve! He applauded and marveled at our success. We were instructed to steal on weekends when it was busy and no one would notice.

This worked for a while, but predictably, his greed grew. Why stop at this amount . . . surely we could steal more? What was the problem? After all, the Arabs he was trying to sell the items to weren't giving him enough money (according to him). Kira and I went to more stores and stole more products. To Mom's, Steve's, and even our own amazement, we easily increased our bounty. Shit, it was amazing!

The ridiculously large bags of merchandise included baby supplies to prepare for Tamara's birth. The sizes of the products grew, like 24-packs of batteries instead of 4-packs, to keep Steve happy.

(Looking back, I know God was with us kids because the things we were able to steal without getting caught were outrageous. We had gotten to the point where we were coming home looking like we had spent a few thousand dollars on batteries, clothing, cameras, household supplies, and more.)

Steve's greed knew no bounds. Instead of making money to buy food, we were funding Steve's dope habit. So we would steal merchandise for him to get him high. This meant we had to go back out again to steal from the supermarkets in order to eat, because he'd always come home with sorry stories about how he had only been able to get twenty bucks for a few thousand in goods. Meanwhile he was higher than a kite all the time.

This streak of luck did not last, of course. The stores had started to notice. After all, we'd been at it an entire summer. They had seen us practically every day, and we'd never left with purchases. So we got caught. A lot! I remember the last time I got caught.

There were so many items that we couldn't carry them alone. We had just stolen bags of goods, and we ran home to have Steve meet us and help us carry everything. After Steve took the goods to sell, I went to the supermarket and ordered some cold cuts and things to eat. I stole some junk for Mom since she was pregnant, and on my way out, I was stopped and pulled into a room in the back.

The police and Mom were called. They arrived simultaneously. They took my picture. Mom begged for them to let me go. After all, all I was doing was trying to steal food for myself and my family. The manager warned me to never go back into that supermarket or they would call the cops. The officers warned us that they would arrest me if I was found stealing again.

So, essentially, I was let off the hook, but Mom cried all the way home. She apologized, prayed, and cried. She had realized that this lifestyle was catching up with her and it was affecting our lives. She told me that I would never be allowed to steal again and that she would try her hardest to fight Steve on the subject. Mom's reality began to weigh on her. She tried talking to Steve about what had happened, but he was too high to listen. That week, Mom called me into her room, crying.

"What's wrong, Mom?"

"I can't take it anymore, Ed." She cried like a baby to me. "Are you strong enough to take care of the kids while I go to rehab to get clean?"

This was huge! I was super excited that Mom was finally going to get clean. I begged her to go. She said that she wanted to, but she feared for my safety. She knew that if she wasn't around, Steve would beat me and take things out on me without her there to defend me. She wouldn't be able to make sure that he didn't go too far. I assured her that if she did it, I would be okay and I would do what I had to do to watch the kids for her.

Mom called a thirty-day rehab and, sobbing the whole time, gave her details to the operator. Then she hung up. It was done! They were on their way to pick her up.

I felt a sense of anticlimax. Our pattern of stealing, Steve getting high, getting caught at the store . . . it was all surreal.

Mom was still scared, though, because Steve was sleeping and had no clue that she was planning to leave for rehab.

After Mom left, Steve woke up, calling for her. "Michelle! Where the fuck is your mother?" When I told him, he flipped out. "Oh, really!"

He looked sad and angry at once. He slammed a few things, left, and returned hours later high as a kite.

11

REHAB
AND
RELAPSE

While Mom was in rehab, I watched the kids, cleaned, and cooked—while Steve slipped in and out of consciousness. When Mom called, he would have us lie to her and tell her that he was getting clean at home while she was getting clean in the rehab. But Mom was smarter than that.

"Just answer yes or no, papi," she would say. "Is Steve standing right next to you?"

"Yes, Mommy, everything is great," I would answer.

"I have a surprise for you," she said one day. "I am clean now, papi, for three weeks. Isn't that great? I love you and promise you it is all going to be over soon. I met this guy named Anthony here, and I like him. We're dating, so I am leaving Steve."

I was so excited. I did not care that she was dating some-one else. I was just excited—and scared shitless—that Mom was almost home.

But before she returned, there was an incident when Steve asked my sister Marisa and me to sleep in the bed with him. He said he wanted me to watch Marisa to make sure she was okay while he slept.

This was a new side to him. I was so anxious for his approval. I was excited. Maybe Marisa had seen this side, but definitely not me. I decided to put my arm around Steve after Marisa fell asleep on the other side of the bed. A few minutes after, I could feel Steve thrusting. At first I didn't know what he was doing and thought he was moving because I had awak-ened him with my arm. But when I went to move my arm from around him, he grabbed my hand and put it on his penis, which was rock hard. This aroused me. I was excited and scared at the same time. At the time I had no concept of morality, him being my mom's husband, or anything like that, and so I responded and grabbed it. He then had me jerk him off until he came.

It never occurred to me that I was the victim—that he was the adult who knew exactly what he was doing.

"Did you like that?" he asked.

"Yes." I was nervous. I was feeling my way here.

"Good, but we can't tell Mom about this, okay?"

I nodded. But then I realized I had to tell Mom . . . Guilt immediately crawled around in my chest. I felt out of breath and a bit overwhelmed. Did I betray Mom? I was a mere child, and I was just happy that Steve and I had had our first "bond-ing" moment.

Finally, he likes me, I thought. How naïve had I been then.

CHOICES

Mom came out of rehab looking great. She was back! We were endlessly excited. Steve was still getting high, though, and her temptation was too much. A few days in, she wanted to leave

Steve, and tried to by having Anthony come over. I remember it like it was yesterday. Mom, Kira, and I all knew the day he planned to come to the house. Anthony came over and knocked on the door. He came into the house and told Steve that he wanted to talk to him. Steve looked scared and confused but said, "Okay, cool," and brought him into the bedroom. We were nervous while we listened in from the other room. He told Steve that he was madly in love with Mom and that Steve needed to leave because he wanted to be with Mom. That dude was bold. He actually had the balls to stand up to Steve!

Then he told Steve that he was going to leave, and when he came back, he wanted Steve gone along with all his shit. Anthony grabbed Mom and started to walk out. Mom paused and held her arm out to us.

"Wait! Let them decide. Are you staying with me or leaving with her?" Steve asked menacingly.

Kira and I looked at Mom in desperation. She said nothing. "Steve," we almost whispered. Something about that fear she had in her face told me that Steve wasn't going anywhere.

Anthony tugged at Mom, and they walked out. Steve flipped out. He charged into the living room and screamed, "I don't give a fuck! I'll kill that nigga—is he fucking crazy!?"

He then grabbed cans of beans from the cabinet and threw them through the window. Afterward he stormed out of the apartment. Kira and I waited, numb with fright. We did not know what was going to happen. One thing was certain, though: No way did we want to spend the rest of our lives with Steve.

He returned alone. Mom came back a few hours later without Anthony. Steve and Mom went into their room and had a conversation, and, of course, Steve and Mom were back at it again. I looked at her sadly. Would it never end? Could Mom not be saved?

"I am sorry, Spaghetti, but I had to come back. I couldn't leave you alone with him."

I was glad she was home but sad things were back to normal.

RELAPSE

And within two weeks Mom was back to getting high on heroin. I can remember Steve yelling at her in the bathroom while they were shooting up. We hated this. It was always the bathroom, then the bedroom! First the bathroom, then the bedroom... Would it never end?

After that, they would "sleep." We had to be silent as mice—tiptoe around or pay the price. Mom and Steve were always either at their methadone maintenance program or in the bathroom getting high. I can remember the arguments.

"Ouch, you missed the vein... Watch what the fuck you're doing!"

"I'm sorry, Steve. Damn, relax! I am not used to this."

It became the norm. Whenever they were out in the living room, Mom was very loving to us. But they were always sick. There was a silent understanding among us kids as to why they were sick—Kira and me more than Marisa, Robert, and Sara. Thankfully, they were too small to know what was going on.

There were times when Steve had only enough money for dope, so he would have me walk with him from 23rd Street and 10th Avenue to 135th Street. Then he would give me a bag of dope.

"This is for your mom. Don't touch it, and don't look at it! Put it in your pocket and walk straight home."

I would then walk back from 135th street to 23rd and 10th and give it to Mom to make her "better." I was a mere child, burdened with the responsibility of enabling my mom's habit.

DIRT

Often Steve took me to do his dirt. He had this Irish friend,

Sean, who was also a dope fiend. He was from a wealthy background and threw it all away because of his habits. Of course Steve was his friend, because Sean had other friends who liked to get high and had money. Steve would turn a profit on Sean's friends, because Steve knew lots of people who would sell to him for cheap. Most of Sean's friends didn't know Steve was reselling to them at high prices.

Sean came over one day bragging about how one of his friends was not street savvy and didn't know anything about pricing. He claimed the guy had lots of money to throw away on dope and pills.

Steve took me with him to meet this guy. All he told me was that the guy had a laptop he was going to give to Steve in exchange for a connection to a drug dealer. So we met this guy on 66th Street by Lincoln Center. The guy looked scared and pleaded with Steve and Sean: "Please, guys, just don't jerk me. I have plenty of money for you guys to get high with me."

"You need to calm the fuck down before I change my mind about this whole deal!" Steve quickly took control. He asked to see the laptop. The guy hesitantly pulled it out, asking not to be beaten or robbed. Steve then asked the guy for the money for the drugs.

"I'm not giving you any money until we get to the spot. I just gave you the laptop." This infuriated Steve, and he handed me the laptop. "You check this out!" He pulled out a knife and stabbed the guy in the stomach and yelled at me, "Run home!"

I started to walk away, and when I looked back, I saw Steve kicking the guy while he was on the ground. That's when I began to run. I was terrified and felt so bad for the guy. I knew we were going to rob the guy, but I had never grasped what that meant. As I ran, the tears poured from my eyes.

With the image of the guy getting stabbed and begging for Steve to stop haunting me, I ran to the lobby of Pops' building, which was nearby. The tenant patrol lady looked at me and asked what was wrong. I was breathless, laptop in hand. She looked at it and looked at me, raising an eyebrow. She knew what was happening, why I was crying.

I got upstairs to the apartment. I saw Mom. I ran to her and hugged her as if I could not let the moment go. I was shaking. She asked me what had happened. I tried to explain, but my nerves were shot. I choked out an explanation.

"That's it, papi. No more. Don't worry. I'm going to talk to Steve when he gets home."

It was a refrain that I had heard so many times before. The regrets. The promises.

Steve arrived few hours later and Mom talked to him about what had happened. He was pissed. He said that I was a fucking pussy and that I didn't even have to do anything but take the laptop and run. He thought he could depend on me. But he knew now I was too soft. He was a master manipulator, playing with guilt and words, making me the aggressor.

He had redefined my self-esteem. The way I saw myself... I hated my body because he drilled in my brain that I was disgusting and had an old man's body at the age of eleven. And every chance he had he called me a faggot or a pussy who was never going to be shit. I was less than a man. It was this kind of mental abuse that redefined my psyche, my self-esteem.

In most situations where self-esteem would make all the difference, I doubted myself because I was always told I would never amount to shit. That I was a fat piece of shit who thought I knew it all but had no clue how to do anything right.

Of course, as an adult, I now recognize it as bullying. I know now that he had to pick on us, on me, for his own self-worth. He was the piece of shit, not me. But all this, the cycle of abuse, of manipulation, the heroin, and my awful responsibility as a child, is only part of the picture. I cannot even recall all the kinds of abuse. This was my life—my nightmare.

12

THE
END OF
CHILHOOD

I recall getting ready for school, and Steve, dope sick,
waking. And I remember the punches, keys jangling, blood
. . . as if it was in slow motion, as if it was happening to
someone else. I heard a sound that was like something from
Super Mario Brothers. The punches, the keys jammed in my
face, a pow sound. I saw a bright white light. I became dizzy,
almost spaced out, rising out of my own body and seeing his
hateful face.

"Go ahead and tell your teacher. Just remember that when
you do, I will go to jail and do my time. But when I get out, I'm
going to kill you."

I mustered some strength and ran to school, crying hysterically. I lined up outside with my class. The kids asked me
what was wrong.

"Be quiet," I hissed. But they persisted. "Mind your own business."

I didn't know I had a huge black eye.

The teacher came to me immediately and said, "Oh, my God, Eddie. You poor thing. What happened to you?"

"Nothing happened. I am fine."

"Eddie, you have to tell me because something obviously happened to you. You have a black eye and you're crying."

I heard Steve's voice and thought to myself, He's going to kill me if I say anything. "Nothing is wrong. I got jumped by a group of boys on my way to school." Would she believe me? She called Mom, who came to pick me up.

TOO MANY ROLES

Then there were those dreaded times I'd be told to take the kids to the park and if anything—"anything at all"—happened to any of them, I would have to answer to Steve. I was also told that if I was smart, I wouldn't even return home in the event something happened to one of the kids. So at this tender age, I was at the park going nuts in fear trying to keep up with all four of the kids. Sara was a baby, so I had to stay by the stroller. Robert and Marisa would run to opposite sides of the park, and Kira was the worst. She had an attitude because she felt that she was too grown to have to listen to me. It was nerve-wracking. I had so many roles: father, big brother, protector. I could not run around chasing a ball. It felt that I had been born old.

Kira would go to the store, disappear, and I was given a hard time. My aunt Janet, who lived in the complex next to us and was often in the park, felt bad for me because I would break down and cry almost every time. None of the kids listened to me and stayed close as I had instructed them to do. I tried endlessly to keep track of each one. Whenever one of the kids would get hurt or cry, the fear of God took over me. I would beg them not to tell Steve about being hurt. This went on every day and stressed me out.

A SIMPLE DREAM

All throughout childhood, I wanted to grow up to be rich to support my mother and family. I was the kind of kid that was very intelligent, had a lot of common sense, and was very sensitive. I'd always dream of how I would get rich, buy a huge house, and put Mom and all my brothers and sisters in there to live.

This was my dream . . . taking care of them until they got old and wanted to move out. Eddie the benefactor. Eddie the caregiver. Eddie the breadwinner.

Mom loved it when I spoke of my dreams. My heart lurched slightly when she gave me that look of pride. I always felt in my heart that she believed I would do it and succeed. No matter what happened, we were always taught by Mom that God had a greater plan for us and that these experiences would be short lived and followed by positive ones.

Even as an adult with a better sense of reality, I am constantly thinking of ways to strike it big to care for us—to watch over my siblings and be the glue that keeps us connected. Mom instilled it in me my whole life: to love unconditionally and to know that we (the family) are, ultimately, all we have.

PART TWO

EDDIE THE TEEN

13

CHILD SERVICES

It was almost impossible to conceive that life could be bad after Steve, away from home. Yet there were other horrors lurking, waiting...

Although I understood none of this at the time, as I was entering my preteen years, several people (including Diane Sawyer, who had observed our family's situation through contact with Kira) filed an official complaint against my mother with the Administration for Child Services (ACS). The original complaint was that my mother was found to be negligent in providing for us because we were at home with a heroin addict while she was giving birth to Tamara.

I will never forget the day we were taken from my mother. Caseworkers from ACS randomly showed up at the Chelsea apartment. Two police officers demanded that Mom hand us over. They explained that the girls (Kira and Marisa) had already been removed from school.

Mom broke down and begged for them to please let her keep us. The entire time we walked to the van that was waiting downstairs, Mom screamed and cried. We began to cry. Mom had just given birth to Tamara and returned home from the hospital. When we got into the van, the ACS worker, Mr.Walker, gave an insincere apology to my mother and ordered the driver to pull out. As we drove away, I watched through the back window.

I was left with an indelible image of Mom on her knees screaming for her children. We were taken to a placement center for ACS on Laight Street. Here there were a score of other kids waiting for placement as well. I was separated from my siblings and put into a group of boys ranging from age eleven to seventeen.

Kira, Sara, and Marisa were placed with girls on the other side of the floor where we had no access to one another. Robert and Tamara were placed on another end of the building with little children. I fought and fought with the staff to be let into the small children's area to take care of Tamara and Robert. Tamara was just a newborn, removed straight from hospital!

I had had so much prior newborn experience that I wanted to make sure she was fully taken care of by me only. I was successful in that. Eventually, the staff became annoyed with my ranting and let me have access day and night to all of my siblings. They explained that this was temporary and we were going to be placed into homes separately. I remember crying to Mom on the phone, telling her that I wanted to run away but couldn't because of the security guards. She cried and asked me to keep the kids together and to be strong. She promised she would do everything possible to get us back. Within two weeks we were placed and separated.

ST. NICHOLAS

The first foster home was at 127th Street and St. Nicholas Avenue in Manhattan. Robert and I had been placed together. It was with a Dominican woman named Grace who had two daughters, a husband, and two other foster children. We lasted about a month. The other kids told me the family fostered for money, and sent it to the Dominican Republic. US money is worth a lot more over there. In her country Grace was practically rich.

We were served disgusting food like unseasoned baked chicken with bread while she and her family ate rice and beans with pork chops and plantains. We were given water while her family had juice and soda. This happened at every meal. I asked to eat what they were eating one night, and I was punished for it.

Whenever I asked to watch TV or leave my room, I was told that if we didn't shut up and comply with the house rules (eating garbage and staying cooped up in our room) then we would face the consequences. Going into the refrigerator was a big no-no!

One day after almost a month of depression, I decided to speak up about the food and unfair conditions we were all facing. One of the foster kids begged me to keep silent. But I refused to accept that I had been removed from my home because of abuse only to be placed in a home where I was abused anyway. So I called the foster mother over and asked her why we were fed in that way and why we were always locked in our room. She told me to shut up or she would call the police to have me removed. I was scared and nervous but stood my ground.

Bravely, I told her to call the cops so we could explain what was happening to us in this foster home. She became extremely aggravated and yelled in my face to shut up and sit down if I knew what was good for me. I said no and then she wailed on me—hitting me in the face and punching me! She called her husband, who came in and yelled at me as well. I started screaming for help at the top of my lungs, because at this point I was scared shitless. She stormed out of the room and called the police. I was excited that she did, because I thought the police were going to rescue me.

After a while the police arrived, but we were locked in our room while she told this bogus story of why they were called. I listened to her rant about me. She explained that I was a foster kid who had mental problems and was always acting out when she was simply trying to provide for us. She wanted me removed.

Another disappointment. No one believed me! The police officers barely listened when I tried to tell them what had just happened. They called me a liar and asked why I had attacked her. I was taken aback. The reality that they weren't there to help me sunk in right away.

I tried to explain that she'd hit me. But Grace had entered the room and showed them scratches on her forearm, stating that it was I who had attacked her. I swore to the cops that she was lying, but they said that I should stop misbehaving—or when I got older, I would wind up in jail. They also said that if I continued to attack her, I would be arrested.

It dawned on me that I was helpless—just another foster child. A problem child. My foster parents were our saviors. I had waited patiently, quietly for someone to listen. When my ACS worker conducted a home visit, I cried my eyes out, begging her to take me from there. She told me that because I was so ungrateful, I was putting my little brother in jeopardy of being put somewhere separate from me. The foster mother was listening to the conversation and burst into the room stating that she wanted me removed because I was teaching the other kids that it was okay to rebel. About a week later, Robert and I were removed and brought back to the Laight Street placement center.

GLEASON AVENUE

The second foster home we (me, Robert, and now, Tamara)

were taken to was on Gleason Avenue in the Bronx. Our new foster mother's name was Winona. Winona's house was not so bad . . . at first.

When we arrived, Winona welcomed me with open arms. She showed me my room where I would be sleeping. The room was amazing! It had a boom box, a treadmill, two windows, a full-size bed—and all of it was mine. Winona was a large, sweet woman who loved to cook. What a difference from crafty, mean Grace!

I was allowed a few hours of free time outside. I would sneak around to see Mom. I would secretly call and visit her every chance I could. I couldn't understand why ACS and all of Steve's family were so against the kids and me being around Mom when all she ever wanted to do was hug and love us.

While living with Winona, I learned a little more about my Puerto Rican culture. She taught me how to master the cooking skills that Mom had started to teach me. I learned how to dance salsa, merengue, and bachata. I also learned where each of the styles of music originated. This was probably the best foster placement I'd had. I got an allowance, was fed great food constantly, and was given things like a beeper for good behavior.

After a couple of weeks, we were also allowed to have phone contact with Mom whenever we wanted. I used my new beeper to have Mom beep me, and I would call her back.

I loved that placement until Selma, Steve's mother, started chatting with Winona, tarnishing her perception of both Mom and me. Selma informed Winona of my younger years when my mother and I stole from her. I admit we did steal from her apartment, but it was for her son! This is why to this day I can't seem to understand Steve's family. They always hated Mom and referred to her as "that bitch" and Kira and me as "that bitch's kids." They blamed us for Steve's addiction.

I'll never understand how people that age (grandparents) could purposely slander a child who was just as much of a victim of their son's madness as they were (and continue to be).

So, slowly we lost the love and support of Winona. Our relationship shifted. She distanced herself, took away my keys to the apartment, stopped letting me have phone calls with Mom, and just began to treat me like Steve and Selma always did: like a bad kid who was a burden and was probably going to steal something.

One day I was in my room and the phone rang. It was Mom trying to speak to me. Winona told her to stop calling because she was now aware of why no one liked us to have contact. When I got pissed off and asked why she did that, she told me to calm down and go to my room. As I walked away, she called Selma, explaining the recent events. She sounded almost proud. It angered and saddened me.

I couldn't take it anymore. I screamed and lashed out. "Why does everyone listen to that miserable, old bitch? My mother is ten times the better person. She's nicer, and she loves me more than you or that old bitch ever will."

"Don't you yell like that, and don't you talk about your grandmother."

But there was no stopping me!

"That's not my grandmother! She hates me because I'm not her real grandson. Don't you get it? She likes keeping us away from Mom because it satisfies her animosity." I kept on yelling. I was beyond anger.

"She loves you and is concerned for you."

This really pissed me off, and my adrenaline was pumping. I had never had an outlet. This free expression was all new. It felt exhilarating, like a weight lifted from my chest. As each second passed, I realized that Steve's family, yet again, had ruined something good for me. My newfound comfort zone was pulled away from me for no legitimate reason, and there was no chance of getting it back.

So I took charge of the situation. I grabbed my belongings and ran away. I got to a pay phone and called Mom crying. I explained what had happened. I got the green light to come downtown to Pops' house to stay for the night. I jumped on the train and headed there. But of course, by the next morning Steve had been informed by his mother that I had called her a bitch, and he flipped out on me. Mom defended me, but he got mad and hit us both.

Just a short while ago, I had been in a safe haven. Now my world was crashing down again.

Mom told me that it would be best to go back to Winona's so that ACS didn't find out I was with her; otherwise, Mom would get into trouble. When I got back, Winona made it very clear to me that because of that episode I was going to be placed in a group home. I didn't say anything as she ranted for hours about me, my mother, and all of the things that Selma had put into her head about us. ACS was contacted, and I was removed maybe two weeks later, after a three-month stay.

14

GROUP HOMES, ROUND 1

After that, us kids were split up. Robert and Tamara
were placed in one home, and Kira, Marisa, and Sara in
another. I was placed alone.

RAHEED

This time I went into a group home on Stephens Avenue in the
Bronx. I was so scared because I had previously heard of group
homes being prime spots for abuse: jail-like settings. When
I arrived I met with a staff member who asked me questions
about myself. He explained the rules of the house. No fighting
or going AWOL. He explained the level system in the house,
meaning our chores, etcetera. I was shown to my room, where
I would bunk with three other guys; in the house there were a

total of about ten guys.

After settling in I was invited to play ping-pong with the residents down in the basement. I was shy at first, but the residents were more than welcoming, especially a guy named Raheed, a tall black dude who looked like a criminal. We played a few rounds of ping-pong before Raheed pulled me into the laundry room area in the basement just a few steps away from the recreation area.

"I want to ask you a question."

"Shoot."

"Never mind."

"Okay."

"Wait."

I looked at him, and he pulled out a note from his pocket. I tried to grab it. He pulled it back.

"Never mind, bro. I just want to tell you that you're a cool dude."

"Thanks, man."

Strange dialogue. I was a little scared. I thought he was setting me up or something. I thought, What the hell was that about? We went back to our ping-pong game.

After a few weeks I adjusted to my environment. I got to see Mom randomly and had phone call rights every week. It was becoming pretty clear to me that I wasn't going back to Mom anytime soon. Most of the children in the home were there because their parents were dead or drug addicts. The staff made it clear that there was a strict system of monthly progressive visitation privileges based around the chore system and adherence to the rules.

One day Raheed asked if I wanted to smoke a blunt. I said I needed to call my mother first. I was really inexperienced at drug use; even though I had witnessed it all my life, I'd never tried anything. He looked confused, and I was oblivious to the fact that it was uncommon for someone to ask their parents if they could smoke marijuana. But I'd always been taught that if I ever wanted to smoke a cigarette, drink alcohol, or try marijuana, that I absolutely had to do it with Mom only. The thinking was, better with her than with someone who could potentially lace it. I called Mom and explained that I wanted to try it and make a new friend. She was taken aback, but she agreed.

"I love you, papi, for being honest with me. You can try it, but I want you to call me right after you do it—and make sure you watch him roll it up. It shouldn't have any white powder of any kind in it, and it shouldn't numb your lips."

I promised to call right after and told Raheed that I would smoke with him. He and I walked a few blocks down from the group home, and he laughed at me for choking on my first pull of the blunt. I was embarrassed but tried to act cool. Raheed then gave me a piece of paper from his pocket, which was that same note from the first night. As I opened it, he warned me not to laugh at him or say anything to anyone else about it. I promised and read the letter, which said: Dear Eddie, I think you're a cool ass nigga and I wanted to know if you would let me suck your toes. Please circle yes or no.

I was shocked, scared, and tried to make light of it. I was also a little uncomfortable because I had never thought about anyone sucking my toes.

"Thanks for the compliment, man, but I can't."

"Why not?" He seemed angry, so I said I'd think about it.

As each day passed, he would randomly ask if I had made my decision. I kept putting it off, but each time he asked, he grew more and more impatient. Until one day, he cornered me!

I was afraid, but also piqued. Oh well, why not?

He grabbed me and pulled me to the bathroom. I thought he wanted sex, so I went to kiss him, but he pulled away. I got nervous, and he instructed me to lie on my stomach and take off my shoes. Then he pulled out his penis. I was aroused and got up to perform oral sex. He let me suck it for just a second and pulled away.

"I don't like that. Just give me your feet," he whispered. He sucked my toes and jerked off until he climaxed.

But afterward he ignored me. He became distant, and refused to speak to me. I was confused. Two weeks later I was in a session with the social worker when she shifted the conversation from family to my sexual preference. I said I was straight and asked why she had asked. She told me that it was okay if I liked men, but I shouldn't express that to the guys in the home because one of them had complained that I was sexually harassing him.

This was a huge shock. He had initiated contact! (I guessed it was my toe sucker.)

"Did Raheed say that he wants to fight me?" She looked at me and asked how I knew she was talking about Raheed. I said it was because he was the only person who could know about my orientation. She looked at me nervously and said that he told her that I'd given him a note asking him if I could suck his dick. I jumped out of my seat and tried to convince her that he was lying. I tried to explain to her that he was the person who had initiated contact from day one. He was outside listening and burst in to attack me. We fought for a few seconds before staff broke us up. For the next few hours the staff called me into a meeting to talk about me and my note. They didn't believe me!

Raheed was downstairs screaming at the top of his lungs that he was going to kill me when he saw me. Naturally I was scared. He was lying. They had confronted me, and now he was ranting!

I was thinking—worrying and anticipating what would happen next. I decided to act crazy. Maybe they would send me back to my mom. I remembered that when Kira had been detained in the Bellevue psych ward, it had been for supposedly hearing voices after the fire-setting incident. So I admitted to writing the note and blamed it on voices I had heard. They were the ones who told me to write the note. Cleverly, I mentioned that the voices were telling me that if I didn't go back home I would hurt someone. I went on to say that the voices also stated that if ACS put me back with my mother, they would stop talking to me.

Needless to say, they thought I was nuts. The staff called in a psychiatrist who worked for the agency to come talk to me the next morning, first thing. He and I spoke about the voices I'd created. He asked me time and time again what the voices would say and how often I heard them. I stuck to my story.

"The voices want me home or they won't go away, and I will have to do bad things to people," I said.

The psychiatrist told me that he was going to take me somewhere safer than the group home and then I could go home. I was excited. I lied and said the voices told me that they were happy and they were going to leave as soon as I was home. But instead the psychiatrist sent me upstate to a mental hospital called Stony Lodge—where I spent the next three weeks realizing what I had just done to myself with my genius plan to get back home with Mom.

At least I was out of the group home. But once more I had become the victim.

15

HEARING
VOICES

At first I believed that life at Stony Lodge would be a new beginning . . . a rebirth.

At the interview I had no idea that I was in a mental hospital. Maybe the ride in an ambulance strapped to a chair should have been my first clue. I met with a psychologist and was asked questions for about an hour. I was reassured that I would be with my mother as soon as I got better.

Better? Implying that I was ill?

Ironically, my roommate actually heard voices. Then I started to panic. I was going to be around a bunch of crazy kids who could lose it at any moment! Ground rules were laid out in my first group session, which was grim to say the least. Can you imagine ten angry kids talking about their experiences and mental illness issues with their parents, school, and so on?

When it was my turn, I decided to be honest. "My name is Eddie Pabon, and I'm not crazy. I just lied about hearing voices so they could put me back home with my mom, and instead they brought me here."

The staff at the group session was annoyed. I was informed that at Stony Lodge the word "crazy" was omitted from all communication.

Okay. So I tried again as instructed. "My name is Eddie Pabon. I just lied about hearing voices so they could put me back home with my mom, and instead they brought me here."

There. No mention of "crazy" . . . better?

But that seemed to piss them off even more. Quickly I was escorted to my room for the night. I was told by a staff member that I wouldn't go anywhere if I continued to resist "the process." The next day I was given medications: Prozac and Thioridazine (an antipsychotic). I refused my meds.

Staff came, and I was restrained and given a shot in my arm that knocked me out cold! Yet every day I would go to group and repeat myself. When the doctors reiterated that all I needed to do to get out of there was be compliant and take my medications, I did exactly that.

So I lied about being insane, and then I lied about being sane. The staff was pleased with my progress and affirmed the participation.

IS SHE FLIRTING?

I learned that even highly medicated kids can find a way to scare each other with sex. One time at dinner, I was sitting with a group of kids far enough away from any adults who could hear our conversation. One of the girls seated across from me smiled and batted her lashes. I was nervous immediately. I remember thinking, Why is this girl looking at me so devilishly? I know she is crazy like all the rest of the kids, so why?

She asked me my name. "Eddie," I blurted out.

"How old are you?"

"Thirteen."

She giggled and leaned over to whisper something to the girl seated next to her. I felt insecure—thinking they were making fun of me or talking about my appearance. After all, I was seriously overweight at this time (about three hundred pounds).

After the girl stopped whispering, her friend said, "She has a crush on you, but you are a little boy. She's fourteen and I'm fifteen. You're not ready for girls like us."

I tried to show off, all the while filled with insecurity and anxiety. "I can handle anybody!"

"Do you know what she likes to do to her boyfriends if she finds out they're cheating on her?" the girl asked.

I shook my head. "What?"

"She likes to ride their dicks and then cut them with a blade or knife."

I tried to play it cool. The other girl looked at me with a scary, seductive smirk affirming what was just said about her. I immediately got up and threw out my garbage and asked to go back to my room for an early night.

When I got to my room, I was scared, replaying what I'd just heard. My roommate walked in and angrily announced that he wanted to go to bed early too. I asked him if he wanted to know what had just happened to me. He said "Why not?" as he tucked himself under his covers.

After I explained, he said, "Dude, that's fucking hot. I would love to fuck her and we'd cut each other up."

Then he proceeded to take out his penis and masturbate until he ejaculated into a napkin while I watched. I was shocked—he was older than I was, about fourteen. Then he just cleaned himself up and went right to sleep as if nothing unusual had happened.

Needless to say, I didn't sleep that night.

ALL BETTER

"Have you heard voices?" It was three weeks in. The main doctor asked me one final time, just to make sure . . .

"Ever since I started my medications, they went away. I feel so much better and want to thank you guys for helping me get better." The doctor said that he would send me back to the group home immediately because the treatment worked. He bought it! After all it was a simple observation that the children who reported "feeling better" consistently would no longer be at group therapy because they had been discharged.

I was so excited about leaving there. I had envied the other kids for having parents who visited them or at least were allowed to do so. I remember calling Mom whenever I was given a phone privilege, and she would cry, asking me where I was. I would also cry and ask her to please come and visit me. She would promise to do so but never made it.

Mom! Mom! I wept silently.

It was only many years later that I found out why. ACS had strictly emphasized to the hospital that Mom was not to be around me under any circumstances. After waiting a while for my release, I was picked up by the same staff member who had brought me there from the last group home. I liked that guy! He was warm and genuinely nice to me.

"Can you adopt me?" I was still incredibly naïve.

"Of course."

But of course he never did. He drove me to my new group home, Marolla Place. On the way he apologized for not believing me about the whole Raheed thing. Apparently after I'd left, there had been further incidents between Raheed and new residents. So now I was more credible. Huh!

I wonder, in retrospect, how did the medications affect me? And how could the staff have believed me? How could I have put myself in that situation in the first place? I was so desperate to escape what I felt were life-threatening circumstances at the group home (and in my real home) that I'd presented symptoms that I'd learned from past experience would get me some sort of help. I knew that I would be taken somewhere safe; I just didn't understand that it would be a psychiatric ward. I often wonder how many other scared children know exactly what to say or do to manipulate their own escape—but don't realize the implications of their actions in terms of the stigma attached to their mental health records or that they may be saddled with an incorrect diagnosis (for the really good pretenders) for the rest of their lives.

At the time, though, it made me smile . . . I must have been a great actor.

SIDEBAR: JOE

My teen years were marked by men, mostly bad ones. So here is an acknowledgment of one of the good guys who tried to help me and my mom.

I remember Joe fondly—so different from all the scumbags I had met. He wanted nothing from us, from me. This made such a difference.

Joe was a ninety-two-year-old man whom my Mom had met through her methadone maintenance program. She went to this program every day at New York Presbyterian on the Upper East Side. There she made a friend named Tina who had bragged about having this rich old man who liked to spend money on her. Mom eventually met him, and he began to give her money, too. Joe was a smooth old man. For a man his age, he had spunk. He smoked cigarettes, drank alcohol, and drove a nice new car.

Tina would yell at him and demand money. So it was Mom who bowled him over. She was nice; Tina acted like a bitch. Joe would say to Mom that he still loved Tina, but Mom was special to him. We (Kira, Mom, and I) would go to his house often in the hope of getting some money. Steve knew about Joe. He had no issue with it. Why would he? Joe had money! So Steve encouraged the situation.

I remember one day Steve asked us to stay over at Joe's house to see if we could find any money lying around. It was eerie and uncomfortable. He had at least thirty photos of mainly deceased family and friends. Included in this parade was his wife of over forty years, looking right through me.

I know what you lot are up to, her eyes seemed to say.

The black-and-white TV stared mockingly at me, too, a symbol of the old, dusty house.

One son worked for NASA, Joe told us, and the other (who didn't care about him) was a successful attorney. He was a bit tired after the storytelling and went upstairs to bed. Mom and I discussed where I was going to look for the money. She followed Joe upstairs, and about ten minutes later, I crept up the stairs. I went into his bathroom where his clothes were, and I found a few fifty- and hundred-dollar bills. Then I went into another room, searched through the drawers, and found a few hundred more. I was so nervous. Adrenaline was charging through my body. I swallowed. What if I got caught? But Steve would be pleased.

The next day Joe woke up and asked if we knew where his money was. We said no, and the poor old man searched everywhere while we helped him look. At the time I didn't feel bad because he was rich. Of course I feel bad now.

I was nervous. He might call the police or something. But he didn't. He just looked at us. He knew. We could tell. But he acted like it was his memory playing tricks on him.

"I guess I must have taken out less money than I thought," he said.

I felt a sigh of relief as he drove us home that day. Mom looked at me with such shame and guilt while in the car, it immediately changed my perspective on what we'd just done. When we got home, Steve was amazed at how much we had taken.

Mom said that she didn't want to do that anymore. Steve promised that he wouldn't have her call him every time we were broke, but eventually he did that anyway. A few days after the money was gone, Steve made Mom call Joe for money. Of course poor Joe came to the house again. When we got downstairs, Joe seemed a little odd. Mom noticed it right away and asked what was wrong, but he dismissed it and said he was just tired. He said he'd been up all night with Tina and needed some sleep.

Mom and I got into the car, and Joe kind of nodded out for a second behind the wheel. Mom panicked and yelled, "Oh my God, Joe!" which woke him up. He swore he was fine and was okay to drive. Mom watched him nervously. He drove on for maybe one or two blocks more before he nodded off again. The car swerved right at the corner of 68th Street and Lincoln Center. Joe ate the red light and drove into oncoming traffic!

The drivers began honking and trying to avoid the car.

"Joe, please wake up, you just ate a red light and we're going to crash!"

He woke up by the grace of God. He drove us back to our building. I was terrified. I had never experienced bad driving before. Mom refused to let Joe drive home, but he insisted. Mom took the keys and asked him what was wrong. He said he was fine, but he had taken a pill from Tina for a headache, and ever since he had been tired. Mom immediately put two and two together and asked him what kind of pill it was. Joe told her it was called Xanax and was a white stick.

Mom was pissed off. She explained to Joe that the medication Tina gave him was extremely strong and could've killed him. Mom suspected that Tina was purposely trying to kill Joe to get his money. Steve was brought downstairs and drove Joe home to Brooklyn.

A few weeks later Mom came home crying. When we asked what was wrong, she said that Joe had died after Tina pushed him down the stairs. I felt my gut drop in that instant! That poor old man was the coolest, most kindhearted guy, and he was killed by a drug addict who only saw him for the next fix.

My feelings about Joe really hadn't hit me until I realized that I, too, was part of the problem. I still feel so bad for Joe and about what I did that night when he went to sleep. If I could see Joe now I'd hug him and thank him for treating us so well and welcoming us into his home. I would apologize and try to explain that I was simply surviving my circumstances. God bless his soul.

I'm sorry, Joe, from the bottom of my heart. I am a man now, and as a man, I sincerely beg for your forgiveness. May you rest in peace forever.

16

GROUP HOMES, ROUND 2

When I arrived at the new group home, everyone was more than welcoming. Overall, the staff was really nice. But of course, even here, I wasn't safe.

EARNING PRIVILEGES

Mr. Walters worked the morning shifts. He brought me into the staff office and explained the rules of the home. He told me that there was a level system just like at Stephens and that I wasn't allowed to leave the home for the next thirty days until I earned privileges. I asked if I could please call my aunt Ella (my dad's sister), whom I had visited with during my foster home experience.

He said I could and so I called. I reached her at work and

asked her for money to have for food and everyday things. While we were talking, I felt Mr. Walters's hand creep up my thigh.

I was both aroused and scared. Why did he think I was gay? Did he? Did the staff brief him about the incident from the last home? Did they know of my sexual orientation?

Did he? Did I?

I was so young and confused, and grappling with life and sexual identity issues. It felt good to be touched in those areas. Looking back, I have nothing but disdain for the adult men who violated my trust and honest cries for male attention. What he did was wrong and unacceptable. I was a minor under his care. But this was far too much for a teen to process.

As the conversation with Aunt Ella continued, his hand went higher and higher. I felt his hand on my penis. I was hard. A green light! There was no stopping now.

As I said goodbye to Aunt Ella and hung up the phone, he locked the door. My heart was thudding. He started taking off his pants. Our eyes were locked as he moved toward me. I pulled off my pants. We gave each other oral sex until he climaxed.

"Don't tell anyone," he said. As if I would!

My "reward" was that I could go see my aunt regardless of the restriction I was on for my first thirty days. So I traveled to her place of work on 149th Street and Third Avenue to pick up the money. It was so good to see her after all those years! She assured me that she would try to be there for me, and I could call her if I needed anything.

Then I called the home and told Mr. Walters that I was on my way. He told me that I needed to hurry back because he wanted me again. When I got there, he immediately locked the staff room and had sex with me. This became a regular thing—almost on a daily basis—when he was on duty. We did it in the basement, upstairs, in the office, living room, you name it!

Well, this affair lasted till Mr. Walters got fired. Not

because of the affair, though. Because he was drinking on the job.

DANNY

A couple of months later, I met Danny. He was an attractive Dominican, and I could not resist him. I had money from doing the most chores and could chip in for blunts, so I started smoking weed with him shortly after he moved in—he was great eye candy and had a flirty vibe.

One day we were hanging out in my room when he told me, "I know something about you, dude, something you may not want to share."

I tried to get him to spill, tell me what he knew.

"Do you like me?" he asked.

"Hell, no, I'm straight, dude."

He laughed and pulled out his dick. "Are you sure, Eddie?"

I grabbed at it instinctively. He pulled away. He said he wasn't gay and wouldn't have sex with me unless I did him a favor.

He wanted me to buy quenepas (a Spanish fruit) from the fruit lady up the block. I walked to the fruit lady and bought them for him. When I returned I locked the door and went to him. He pulled out his penis and asked me to suck it. I did for a few seconds, but he told me I wasn't doing it right. He then tried to penetrate me. That didn't work either because I couldn't handle the pain, so he got mad. He said that I needed to learn how to have sex, and until I did, he wasn't feeling it.

I left the situation alone after that because that wasn't the first time I'd been told that. I felt stupid for not knowing how to perform oral or anal sex. I remember asking myself what was wrong with me. Why couldn't I do anything right?

One night I was hanging out with some of the guys, smoking a blunt, when Arnold (one of the troublemakers) burst into the room and started teasing me. "Eddie's a faggot! Eddie's a faggot!"

"What the fuck are you talking about?" I asked.

"Danny told me you tried to suck his dick. That's mad gay!"

Embarrassed, I jumped up and acted surprised to the other guys. I went over to Danny, who was laughing. I asked him to verify that he had said that about me.

"Why don't you tell them the whole story?" I said.

"I did."

At that point I knew that I had to fight him to prove that I wasn't lying—it wasn't the whole story! After all, he had started it with the "I know your secret" shit. I grabbed a pencil and swung at his face to stab him. I missed. He swung a blow to my face. He was way bigger and older (nineteen), and I basically got my ass whooped. The fight was broken up, and the staff on duty forbade us to be next to each other.

The next day Danny was transferred to another group home with guys that were around his age.

DAILY NEWS

It was during this time that Mom and Steve decided to sell our story to the Daily News, National Inquirer, and anyone else who would pay them. On a phone call, Mom said that she was making thousands of dollars telling her story to these media people.

Their story was that Diane Sawyer had offered her a few million dollars to adopt Kira so that she could give her a better life, and when Mom had refused, Diane had called ACS on us. I did not believe it. Not any of it. Come on, it was bullshit! Mom said that I didn't have to believe the story, but it was the truth. She asked me to tune in to some show at six o'clock that day. I rounded up all the staff and my friends at the group home and tuned in.

To my surprise, there were Mom and Steve crying on television. Is this true or is it a scheme to get money? I thought. All the guys in the group home went nuts when they saw my mother.

"She is hot!"

"Damn, Eddie, can I holler at your mom?"

The next morning I was riding the train to school and looked over at a man holding a newspaper. The front page said: "Diane's Secret Little Girl." I got excited. Not about the content but about the picture of Kira at Diane's ranch on the front cover.

"That's my sister!" I yelled. "Hey, mister. Can I please buy that paper from you . . . please?"

The man and other passengers looked at me, confused.

"I swear that's my sister, and the story is about my family. Please!"

The man handed me the paper, and I read the story over and over. It painted such a ridiculous picture. The story said what Mom was saying but also included bogus facts, like the part where I had been arrested several times since being removed from her custody and had dropped out of school.

I had never been arrested and was on my way to school! I was offended and embarrassed. The world thinks I am a criminal.

When I got off the train, I called Mom and asked what that was about. She apologized and said that the paper thought it would sell more copies if they included all those things. She said they got paid $5,000 for the story.

"So, are you guys getting your life together to take us back now that you have money?" .

"Papi, you know Steve took the money and spent it all already. We just got a notice from NYCHA that we are being evicted. We are losing the apartment here. We are going into the shelter system."

As she began to cry, I got frustrated and angry. "You know, Mom, I am getting tired of you staying with this man after everything he put us through. We are waiting for you guys to get it together and get us out. Please, Mom, leave him. You don't need him. I will take care of us."

"Papi, you are too young. I have nobody else. I promise I

will get better and get you out."

But the media attention faded as fast as it came. I never believed the story, to be honest. Kira and I have talked to Diane about this, and she writes it off as being lies. She simply fell in love with a little girl who she deemed in need of a support system. She is committed to being a support to her and for that I am grateful to Diane.

17

HOPE
AND
BETRAYAL

Months turned to years. It felt like I was at Marolla Place forever. I begged my aunt Ella to please take me into her home. She went through the court proceedings and eventually obtained custody of Kira and me. In the meantime, Selma was fighting for custody of all of Steve's kids.

Living with Aunt Ella was great at first. We got that homey feeling, with good food and family comfort, and since it was Titi Ella, we felt wanted and loved. She had two children, Felix and Vanessa. Her place was a two-bedroom apartment, where we all had to share one bedroom and my aunt had her own bedroom. I was happy to be reunited with Kira, and things were looking up overall. We developed a routine where I cooked, cleaned, and baby-sat while my aunt worked. I didn't mind this, and there were no issues.

Then it changed. Suddenly we were just extra mouths to feed. It was thrown in our face every time my aunt was in a bad mood. My uncle Hector, who lived in the neighborhood and was someone I'd stay with occasionally, informed my aunt that I was smoking marijuana with some friends I had in his building, and my aunt began to pick at everything she could to get rid of me. If we were watching television and Vanessa or Felix wanted to watch something else, we were told that it was their apartment and we had no say. She also demanded that I go get a job since I was old enough (fifteen) to work. She would say things like, "You think you're going to just sit around here doing nothing on my budget?" It was tense all the time.

I went job hunting and found a job giving out flyers for a tanning salon in Midtown. I was so excited. I thought that if I stopped smoking and worked part-time, my aunt would be proud of me. When I got home and told her that I had found a job, she became furious and asked who I thought I was getting a job when I had school. I showed her that the hours were for the weekend and it wouldn't interfere with school, but she forbade me to work.

Her reasoning was that I needed to be available to baby-sit on the weekends and to concentrate on school during the week. With each day that passed, the stress continued to build with my aunt. I never disrespected her or talked back, yet she would rant about how sneaky we were. I will admit, I knew she had a stash and would take a dollar or two here and there. She knew I was doing this, and it didn't help the situation get any better. I could sense it was a matter of time before I was going to get kicked out. After all, I was used to it. By this time it had become a pattern. People changing on me, and life turning rotten.

Felix's father, Donald, had been in prison for most of the time Kira and I had resided in my aunt's house. But he was released right around the time we started having issues with my aunt. After he was briefed on the custody situation, the plans to get rid of me went into full effect.

I think that my aunt had just grown tired of the heavy

responsibility of taking care of us. So she contacted ACS to have me removed as soon as possible. I was despondent over this, because I felt that I had complied with all her wishes. I did everything by the book! But in spite of this, I was still viewed as a burden. It seemed as though the whole dynamic changed overnight. Prior to and after Donald's release I was always respectful, cleaned up after myself, did well in school, cooked when given the opportunity to, and was humble in every conceivable way to earn my stay.

But immediately after his release, Aunt Ella's fuse became shorter. She was impatient and annoyed. She told me that Donald didn't like me because I was "a bad, unappreciative kid."

And so I was moved to Uncle Hector's, though Kira was allowed to stay with Ella. Ella and Donald took the kids to live with Donald's family in the Bronx. Granted, the only reason Kira was able to stay with them was because my aunt used Kira's SSI check to pay for Vanessa to go to private school. And then there was Kira's connection to Diane Sawyer, which had potential. This was the way it seemed.

Meanwhile, my uncle Hector was pissed that he'd gotten stuck with the responsibility of taking care of me. So there was no homey feeling at his place! It was bad from the beginning. Once again I was told that I was a burden. I started to smoke marijuana heavily with the kids in the building again. Having friends was my way of dealing with the emptiness I began to feel, especially since my home life was so stressful.

I was being rejected yet again. My self-worth continually declined.

When I cleaned my uncle's apartment, he would say it wasn't good enough. If I took a bath, he'd say I used too much soap. When I did the dishes, he would say the same thing. The list goes on and on.

A SAFE SPACE . . . YEAH, RIGHT

After about six months I accessed a clinic at school where mental health services were available. Then I started talking. I always looked forward to meeting with my therapist.

A free period from class and I got to hang out with my therapist—this was really fun. Finally it was about Eddie. About home, about the guys I had been with. About Kira. About Mom. About Steve. And finally I could be open about my feelings without consequences! Not once did they change their minds, and there was no beating to follow.

Yes, this was an inviting environment. My therapist had no negative reactions when I expressed myself. I truly loved my therapist like a best friend and trusted her. If I had sex, I told her with whom, and how it was, just as if she was my mother.

I had been informing her of my aunt's situation from the time I was kicked out to stay with my uncle. In each session she would be updated on my home life. One day I was talking about Donald and how when he was released, all of the home life changes had come into effect. I told her about him not liking me and made the mistake of informing her that he had slapped Felix in the face for a stupid reason. Felix was five at the time and was slapped for having a tantrum. What I didn't know was that therapy sessions are confidential until reports of abuse or illegal activities are mentioned. At my next session, about a week later, my therapist's supervisor asked for my aunt's contact info. When I asked why, the therapist looked at me differently. Like she felt bad for me and was about to drop a bomb. She said that she had called ACS and needed to call her in to talk with her about what I had reported.

I became scared. No more confidentiality. What would happen if aunty found out I had ratted Donald out unintentionally? So I covered up. I said that what I had said originally was a lie. By then it was too late. There was also going to be a group session. I was invited by my therapist to tell my aunt about my sexuality when we all met. I was hesitant. Yet what could happen? After all, this was meant to be a safe place. So I agreed.

I thought it would be perfect because she couldn't hit me

(not that she ever did, but I always imagined it happening if I told her I was gay). My aunt came to school with me the following Monday, and we met with the therapist. She opened the floor for me to tell my aunt about my sexual preference. I did, and my aunt looked shocked. Then the therapist took over and mentioned the incident of Felix being slapped. She also informed her that the supervisor called in a case on her.

Naturally, Aunt Ella denied it, got pissed off, and when the meeting was over, she took me directly to ACS. During the entire train ride Donald looked at me like he wanted to kill me. My aunt repeatedly let me know that I was cut off for life.

They ranted and raved, saying they felt like beating the shit out of me for what I did. My aunt embarrassed me on the train.

"I don't care if you want to be a little faggot . . . you don't fuck with my kids."

I looked around. People were staring. Then I just broke into tears. I regretted ever telling her the truth. Now it was being used against me. Imagine . . . I opened up about my life and feelings only for my world to be rattled yet again. After this experience, I swore off any kind of therapy again, for fear of bringing on consequences.

Consequences I'd thought I was finally free of.

18

CONFESSIONS

Mom would read the bible with us and have a bible study from time to time, where we would take turns reading the bible together. As children, we were always in and out of different churches and had a lot of spiritual connection with God. We prayed in random Catholic churches, were baptized by Mormons as children, learned about Jehovah's witnesses, and just praised God regardless of what our religion was.

During our disastrous stay with Aunt Ella, Mom took us to a Pentecostal Christian church. Kira had made a friend whose mother was seriously religious. Kira met the girl at her Catholic school and went to church with her whenever she could. At first Kira was going on her own, but eventually after being invited, Mom decided to have us go with her. Mom, Kira, and I went to the church, and I was introduced to a whole new experience with religion.

Kira told me about people speaking in tongues and receiving the Holy Spirit, but I didn't believe it till I saw and heard it. Speaking in tongues is supposed to be the language of God, and there are two types of people: people who can't speak it but understand it and people who can speak it but don't understand it. When we stepped into the church and the service started, people began to sing and dance and then boom, there were a few people whose eyes rolled back while they lost control of their bodies. It was explained to me that when that happened, you were literally being lifted by angels and given the feeling of release for a moment just before coming back into your body. I didn't believe this until it was my turn to step up to the priest. He introduced me and patted me on the head. Instantly I felt light-headed and my body got lighter, but I was so worried about being embarrassed in front of the people who were watching me.

Don't give in, don't look stupid, Eddie, please God no. I opened my eyes, and the priest looked at me as if he knew I was resisting. I continued to fight it in my thoughts, and he walked away from me while shaking his head in disappointment.

Mom was told that she had demons in her, and a few people gathered around her to pray and remove them. Mom's whole demeanor changed. It was scary. She looked at them as if she was angry while they all prayed around her. She jumped up and screamed, "Nooooooo!"

The church people continued to pray until she came back to herself. We were sold. I believed in God more than ever from that moment on. The fact that Mom became a whole different person while they were praying was evidence enough for me. The whole time after that experience I was mad at myself for not letting go and to this day I wish I would've. When we got into Kira's friend's car, the lady who brought us there said to me, "You didn't let go and that's not good. You have to let God take over." After she said this to me, I became even more spooked because I couldn't understand how the hell she knew I was resisting.

We went to her apartment, and Kira, her friend, and I were in the room talking about stuff when the subject of me being gay came up. I had just told Kira a few days before and sworn her to secrecy. Kira said that I needed to be honest and tell Mom, so I went to tell her. When I got into the living room, I found the girl's mother and Mom talking about God, and the woman was speaking in tongues. In that moment, when I was in the woman's view, she paused, looked up, and closed her eyes. When she opened them she looked at me and said that God had told her that I needed to tell Mom something very important. She assured me that she was right and that it was up to me to let go or not.

After hesitating I told her that I was gay. Mom was shocked but told me that she loved me no matter what. She already had an idea, she said. (After all, I had tried to come out when I was a kid . . .) The lady then said to me that I had another secret that God told her about that I needed to tell Mom.

Immediately, my stomach turned because I knew that this was it! I had to come clean to Mom. After hesitating, I dropped the real bomb and told her that Steve and I had had sex. I begged her not to tell him anything for fear of being beaten to a pulp for opening my mouth. She assured me that she loved me unconditionally and she wouldn't say anything to him. She spent the next hour absorbing what I'd just revealed to her. When it was time to leave, she hugged me and told me that she loved me no matter what. While we were on the train, she looked at me and asked me to go into detail about what happened. I did. I told her everything.

Obviously, Mom was in shock and was processing everything. She cried for a second and told me she didn't know what to do. I begged her not to say or do anything because I didn't want either of us to get hurt.

"What am I supposed to do, Ed? I have to sleep next to this man, this monster. I love you, papito, and I want you to know that what he did was wrong."

I apologized and asked her to understand that I had as much fault as he did because I was engaging in the acts more than willingly.

We got to Pops' house, and as Mom promised, she never said anything about it to him. It took me a long time to understand that I was the child, the victim!

19
ONE STEP FORWARD, TWO STEPS BACK

After my aunt dropped me off at ACS, I was taken to a new group home, St. Peters in the Bronx. This time I was still scared but used to the constant moving. I was comforted, too. It was a place I had experience with—another group home. When I arrived I was given the routine rundown of the rules. This group home was attached to another group home so instead of there being twenty guys, there were forty. I was about fifteen at that point. I had met with a job coach who assisted me in getting my working papers and finding my first job at White Castle on Westchester Square. I loved it. I was young and employed.

Wow, I have a freaking job! This is cool, I thought.

TRUTH OR DARE

It was at White Castle that I met my new best friend, Samantha. She and I hung out every chance we had. We smoked blunts, drank, and talked about men. Samantha lived with her mother, who was in the army, so we hung out in their house often. It turned out that Samantha's mother shared Mom's birthday, and her stepfather at the time shared Steve's.

In addition, we were both Cancers and were both born on the same day as one of our uncles. It was those random small similarities that brought me to my first time experiencing a long-term friendship.

To avoid being at the group home all day, I chose to hang out with Samantha. At the time I had a huge crush on this boy Juan. He lived in the group home next door and was always nice to me. One day we were hanging out in the basement and wrestling while he was in his sweatpants, and I grabbed his penis. He jumped back and asked why I did that. I lied and said that it was a mistake. We continued to wrestle, and I got hard.

But I felt the vibe! I knew he was sexually interested in me. He felt my penis and paused and looked at me. He said, "Yo! What the fuck was that I just touched?"

"Nothing." I was nervous.

"Nah, that wasn't nothing. Are you gay, bro?"

"I am not! You are bugging out, nigga, relax," I said defensively.

He gave me a hug and walked away. I was nervous. I had been down this road too many times. I wondered what he was going to do or say. But he said nothing.

The following week he approached me again in the basement to wrestle. I knew he was interested. I acted nonchalant and wrestled with him. Every chance I got I would try to "wrestle" with Juan (lol). One day he approached me in the basement to . . . give him head.

I laughed it off, but he was serious and pulled out his penis. Of course I didn't hesitate and went right to business. He loved it! We agreed to keep it quiet and really didn't do much reflecting. The one time I tried to speak about it, he cut me off midsentence.

"Wanna be the bitch in the relationship?"

"Bitch? Fuck you, nigga! I ain't nobody's bitch!" I laughed.

"You wanna be my bitch?"

"Hello! No!" He quickly responded.

No bitches. It was agreed! Both would be the men. And we would not talk about it! Fuck, it was awkward for both of us. Also, he had a girlfriend whom he would ditch to hang with me.

I told Samantha at work the next day. All this juicy news! So much to share! Samantha didn't believe me. She'd met his girlfriend. So we made a bet that I could prove it to her within three weeks or I would have to give her $50. He was a closet case, but I was sure that with the right amount of marijuana and alcohol I could prove it to her. As Juan and I hung out more, we did everything together. We even snuck into each other's rooms at night to cuddle.

One day we were smoking a blunt with Samantha. "Let's play truth or dare," she said. All part of the plan! Juan was practically my man, but we were totally discreet. Juan went first.

"Kiss Eddie," he told her. She did. My turn.

"Kiss Samantha," I said.

Then Samantha asked for me and Juan to make out. He gave the typical straight guy response. "Nah, nah, man, that's homo. I ain't doing that!"

We assured him that whatever happened would stay between us, and no one would ever find out. We said that if he kissed me, it wouldn't make us gay. So with a little hesitation on both of our parts, we made out. As the game went on, we progressed to touching and then grabbing each other's privates. I had pretty much won the bet, but Samantha wanted more proof. She felt that it was just a truth or dare thing.

For the next few days, I tried picking up the pace a bit. We went to Samantha's house for some drinks. We had a few shots of vodka while she was ironing and not paying attention to us.

"Pull out your dick right here and let me suck it in front of Samantha," I whispered in Juan's ear.

"Yo, you are crazy." He smiled cynically. "Go ahead, do it!" He placed his arms behind his head and lay down on her bed. I pulled out his penis and gave him a suck or two while kicking Samantha with my leg to get her attention. It worked!

"Ohhhhhhh, myyy Gooooodddddddd! What are you two doing? Stop that before my mother walks in here and catches you!"

Juan was a little embarrassed but brushed it off, and we continued to hang out that night as if nothing ever happened.

Sadly, Juan and I eventually stopped hanging out because people in the group home were starting to question our closeness. Even his girlfriend wanted to know why she was always being blown off all the time for me.

THE HEIST

A few months into my stay at the home, I began to mingle with the older crowd and was asked to start selling marijuana for one of the residents. I accepted the offer and became the new dealer for the neighborhood. After selling for a while, I noticed that I was making much more money selling drugs than working at White Castle. Soon I lost my job anyway, because for two days, being young and stupid, I didn't show up to work or call in.

After becoming the new dealer, I felt like I needed to prove that I was tough and could keep up with the older guys. So I did stupid things. One morning I attempted to rob the safe of the home when no one was around. The other residents were hyping me up to do it. I was willing, too, because I'd seen a staff member place a few hundred dollars in there the night before. I grabbed a fire extinguisher and slammed it against the lock of the cabinet where the money was. I banged it over and over until it broke. To my surprise there was a measly seven dollars in the cabinet.

All this shit for a few dollars!

I didn't know what to do nor did I plan or think about what would happen afterward, so I ran away. I felt stupid. I tried to go to various family members' homes to stay. But I appeared to have no options. So I returned to St. Peters and was placed instead in the Popham group home, where things took a turn for the worse.

THE GOING GETS TOUGHER

Popham . . . the true definition of troubled kids.

It was the home where the agency sent all the kids who were bad in other group homes—and now I was one of them!

Most of the guys were about to max out of the group home system at twenty years old. I was the youngest kid there. The guys were constantly being locked up for beating people up. They robbed people, didn't have any family, and were just lost souls trying to survive. They'd spent so many years in the system hopping from place to place and being institutionalized. Now I, too, had become a statistic.

I thought that doing stupid shit to impress them was the way to get by. This worked initially but eventually was my downfall. I stayed there for about two months before I had to leave. I was doing things like having water fights with fire extinguishers and fighting staff. I began to cut classes a lot in school. I copied the others. I did pretty much whatever I wanted. But it backfired one fine day. Everyone was placed on restriction with no privileges at all due to my stunt with the fire extinguishers. The other guys didn't like that, and I got word from a housemate that they were planning on jumping me that night to teach me a lesson. I packed my shit while no one was looking and left.

Again, I felt stupid. I was beginning to realize that the criminal life wasn't for me. I didn't fit in with the misfits, but neither did I fit in with "normal" kids my age. I just did not fit in anywhere.

And so I ran away to live with Mom and Steve at a shelter on 135th Street and Lenox.

Back with Steve? Seriously? What was I thinking?

20

SCOOBY

While I was in and out of group homes and Pops' place, I started using phone chat lines to meet guys. The strangest and scariest encounter I had was with a guy named Scooby when I was just fifteen.

I was watching TV one night when I saw an advertisement for meeting men on a phone chat. So I called and set up an account. Phone chat lines were an easy route to finding hookups, I learned.

One day I went to a live one-on-one connection with a man named Scooby. How old are you? You were supposed to be eighteen to use the chat line, and I was only fifteen. So I lied. Seventeen, I said.

We arranged to meet at his apartment in the Bronx. I traveled over to Allerton Avenue on the 2 train. I was greeted by a big, tall black guy who scared me. He looked at me like I was a piece of meat.

He brought me into a bedroom, where I met "Scooby." Scooby told me he wanted to teach me how to serve a man so I could be good at it when I got older. I was scared and aroused. I didn't know what to expect, and all I kept thinking of was the big black guy outside the door. I did not like the vibe at all and wanted to leave but didn't know how to.

I sat on a chair that was placed beside his bed. He removed his pants and came over to me in underwear—I could see his penis was hard. He grabbed my face and pushed it into his penis and rubbed it all over my head. He said he wanted to fuck me. I was really scared at this point because my prior experience with sex never had included any form of anal intercourse.

I told him that, and he assured me that he would teach me the right way to take a penis in my ass. He promised me it wouldn't hurt. I removed my clothing and followed his instructions. He had a huge penis, so I was definitely more scared a this point. He tried for the next few minutes to put it in me but was unsuccessful because I kept weeping for him to stop.

After a few more tries, he got frustrated and told me the least I could do for him was suck him off. I tried to, but I was too inexperienced to do it to his liking. He became even more frustrated and grabbed me and told me to stand there while he jerked off. He eventually ejaculated all over my face and asked me if I liked it. I said I did, and he asked if I wanted to try to put it in me again. I didn't, and I said so. He got a little angry and aggressive and told me I had better learn to start taking it or he would force me to learn. He asked me my age, and again I said I was seventeen.

"I know you're lying to me about your age. I'll tell you my age if you tell me yours."

He showed me his New York State ID. The dude was about forty-five. I was in shock. He'd said twenty on the phone. I told him I was really sixteen, which was still a lie. He has said he would keep my age a secret if I kept his a secret. We hung

The Son Will Rise In December 111

out for some time in his room talking and feeling each other. Scooby then looked at me with an evil grin.

"I'm hungry, and if you know what is good for you, then you will heat up some food."

When I asked what would happen if I didn't, he told me he would get his black friend to teach me how to take a monster-sized penis, whether or not I was ready.

This horrified me, but I felt trapped. I'd come to this stranger's apartment. What did I expect? I couldn't make a dash for it. What if I struggled with the door? Surely they would stop, rape, and kill me. So I walked cautiously to the kitchen and heated up some food I found in his refrigerator. When I opened the fridge, I noticed that he had a case of Ensure supplement drinks. According to the label they weren't for resale. I knew then that he had a medical condition. I could remember Mom had told me that Ensure was prescribed to people with health issues. At this point I was terrified, so I said that I needed to call home or I would get in trouble. Scooby didn't like this and looked bothered.

"I absolutely have to or my mom might call the police, and be scared that something might have happened to me."

I pretended to call home after he gave me permission and acted like Mom was so mad at me that she demanded that I go home. I told him that I could return the next day.

He let me leave, and I ran to the train.

I was crying, running, and thanking God for letting me make it out of there alive. I received messages in my mailbox after that from Scooby asking that I call him and come back to complete my "lessons." I deleted that account. That was the end of him!

21

SHELTER LIFE

Going to live in the shelter with Mom and Steve was a big mistake! This shelter wasn't for me nor was it okay for me to stay there, but the staff feared Steve and let me stay anyway.

The room we were staying in was small, very small. Steve's drug use was getting out of hand. By then he was into "double banging," shooting up with both coke and dope. He would wake up in the morning livid. He'd slam shit, curse out the staff, and threaten us. It was classic Steve being Steve. I can see it as if it was yesterday. He would come home shaking, thirsty for his hit.

He'd pull out his needles, plastic strap, spoon, and lighter. He would cook the coke first so he didn't fall out before the next hit. He even gave me a tutorial on how to shoot up.

So you put the coke in the spoon and a few drops of water. Then you use the lighter on the bottom of the spoon to cook it till it boiled a little. Then you put a cotton ball in it and use the needle through the cotton ball to filter while sucking it into the needle. Then you find a good vein and shoot.

After he did coke and dope, his paranoia kicked in. He would light a cigarette with his eyes wide open, twitching and shaking, and he would stare out of the peephole for hours until it wore off.

When we asked why he was staring like that, he said that he was looking out for the detectives because they were coming for him. (By that time Steve had been on the run from the DA for years . . . the same one who had organized the witness protection program after the dirty DA had been ousted.)

We loved when he was high because it meant that we could stop worrying about being randomly beaten or screamed at. Yes, even at this late stage, Steve still had the power to instill fear!

Mom was still getting high, but I never viewed her as a drug addict. From my teenage perspective, my mom was simply trying to get better so that she wouldn't be sick anymore.

Though it was good being out of the homes, the living situation with Steve and Mom lasted only a few months. As usual, Steve's need to feed his addiction interfered with every good thing that came my way.

WESTERN BEEF

Mom and I were out walking one day, and we bumped into an old friend who knew Dad and his girlfriend Joanna from back in the days when they were younger. This woman worked at Western Beef on West End Ave, near Pops' building. After she and Mom caught up on old times, I mentioned that I needed a job and asked if they were hiring.

She offered to refer me for a cashier's position. As the conversation progressed, Joanna was mentioned. She gave us Joanna's number, and we called right away. Joanna was at work, a few blocks away. We gave her the address of our shelter, and she came over immediately to see us. When she arrived she told us about her new man and their son. She told us that they were well established, both drove BMWs, owned a nice home, and stuff like that. From that time on I made sure I visited   Joanna as often as I could at her work to keep in touch. I guess she reminded me of Dad. I felt good being around her.

Working at Western Beef was such a blessing at the time. I made about $250 a week, way more money than I needed at sixteen. I did my job, and I did it well. The job was only a few blocks away from Pops' house, and that was pretty convenient. Everything was going well until my first check came, and Steve's greed reared its ugly head. He wanted a big cut of my pay—half—for helping out with bills. Say what? What bills? For heaven's sake, we were staying in a shelter. It started off with half my pay, then all! After a month or so of working to support Steve, I began to think of ways to make money that he couldn't take. I figured if I made extra money and he wasn't aware of it, then I could pocket the money. Having the experience that I had stealing from everywhere else, I learned how to steal from the register at work without coming up short.

This became my secret pay that Steve didn't know about. I rationalized the behavior by looking at it as though I was helping my community and making money at the same time. I would see poor families come in at the beginning of the month when government-issued checks came in (SSI and welfare), and they'd shop their checks away. The way I made my money was that I would not charge them for the expensive goods. I just charged them fifty dollars for myself. For example, if a customer brought $500 worth of groceries, I would only ring up $250, charge my fee, and still save them $200.

Naturally, the people who shopped there loved this. Even the rich people in the neighborhood loved me. The only problem was that after doing that for a few months, there would be lines to the back of the supermarket for me while other cashiers were saying, "Next customer, please. We're open, too!" And the entire line all had full shopping carts. It became clear to management that I was doing something fishy, and I was fired immediately.

THE ULTIMATUM

After I got fired from Western Beef, I packed bags in the supermarket across the street. There I made about thirty dollars a day—twenty dollars on bad days. Steve knew what I was making, and it was budgeted for before I even came home.

I was to give him twenty dollars to get a dime of coke and a dime of dope, and I could keep the remaining ten, assuming there was anything left over. Giving him money for his shit pissed me off, but it kept him from beating us.

As each day passed, Steve got worse. It was a given that he would wake up furious, because he was withdrawing. The money I was making was becoming more and more Steve's coke and dope money. I woke up one morning, and he flipped out, punching me in the face and yelling at me to go work for money. Then he left.

Mom and I were crying together, and I gave her an ultimatum. Either we leave Steve and I would take care of us or she should just stay with Steve and I would leave. Mom looked sad.

"I want to leave with you, papito, but to what and where? We don't have anything. And how can you take care of me?"

I felt stupid and less than a man because I couldn't take Mom out of that situation. She was right. I packed bags, for Christ's sake. How was I going to support her? This was the second time I tried to save her and it didn't work. So I apologized to her and explained that I would be leaving on my own.

But where? Joanna came to mind. I called Joanna and begged to live with her until I got on my feet. I explained what was going on at home, and she offered that I baby-sit the kids (James and Emmanuel) after school during the week while she worked. In exchange I could live with her. I left and moved in with Joanna, Marco (her man), James (my paternal brother), and Emmanuel (Marco and Joanna's son).

At this point, I was kind of mad at my mom because I felt betrayed. While I understood where she was coming from, I felt like she picked Steve over me. I decided to teach her that I was serious about changing my life. So I chose to have no communication with her while living with Joanna and Marco.

22

NEW REALITY, NEW AWARENESS

I knew from the beginning that my time with Joanna and Marco was limited. How long before the bubble burst, before they got tired of me?

They insisted that I could stay. But I had lived with every family member, besides all the group homes. And it had all ended badly.

So I went through the motions. I told them I would get a job and be out within the year. Of course they objected. This was the "honeymoon phase," during which Eddie was the best and could do no wrong.

For the first three or four months, I was a kind of live-in nanny. It was amazing and life-changing. The scene was so different. It gave me a new perspective. They were rich!

During the first week Marco gave me three pairs of Nike

sneakers. Three! I had never had more than one pair of Payless shoes at a time. I was so grateful and began to get comfortable. They had a huge TV, a game room with the latest PS2s and computers, two floors, and a front yard and backyard. This house was like something from a movie. I would watch my brothers after school until Joanna and Marco got home, from Monday to Friday. But babysitting was the most fun experience. I would get up early and send the kids to school. I stopped smoking marijuana because Joanna and Marco didn't like that, and I didn't want to mess things up. After everyone left the house, I would blast their Bose surround-sound system and clean the house. I made sure the house was always clean. In the beginning they were impressed by my efforts. They loved it. And I did all the work for them. I dusted, vacuumed, took out the trash, and sometimes prepared dinner. They would leave me money for food to take the kids to McDonalds or to any activities that were planned.

It was there that I realized that at almost three hundred pounds, I needed to lose weight. I started a diet and lost a hundred pounds by eating McDonalds McSalad Shakers and water all day for about six months. I thank God for the experience I had there because I learned what it was like to live a different kind of life. I learned that there's more than just surviving, stealing, selling and using drugs, and just being ghetto.

I watched Marco and Joanna work. They became my role models. They had it all—Gucci and Rolexes—and I wanted what they had. Things were great.

TIME'S UP

But as I'd predicted, after a while the honeymoon was over. The familiar cycle emerged. Joanna began to change, accusing me of lying about having cleaned up. She was the type of person who would take out her minor frustrations on me or the kids.

At first, I knew Marco had my back and knew that I was

a good kid. He defended me when she yelled. Then he, too, yelled at me. And nitpicked. Soon my time would be up.

I continued to clean, do laundry . . . whatever it took to prevent their dissatisfaction and disapproval. It was useless. They'd find something, guaranteed. Then came the restrictions . . . suddenly I could eat only certain things. Other things were for the kids only.

Once again there was a vibe, a certain discomfort. Once more I was reminded that this was not my home. I had been so used to getting by on less and having restrictions—so what was new?

Joanna came home one day, and in the middle of her ranting, she said that I needed to start looking for a job because I needed to get my shit together and move out. I hadn't spoken to my mother in months by that point and decided to call her to touch base just in case I needed to go back to the shelter with her. Speaking to my mother again was refreshing and reminded me that no matter what happened, I would always love and have her unconditionally.

Mom cried when I called her. She was so surprised to hear from me. Mom loved and missed me and understood why I stayed away. She assured me that if I needed to go back, she would be more than happy to have me back again. I surprised Marco that day. I apologized for being a burden to them, and he seemed confused.

"I'm going to get a job fast, and eventually, I will leave here. I just need three months to save up money."

He got mad and asked why I was saying this to him. I explained what had happened earlier with Joanna, and he apologized to me for what she said. He told me that he didn't want me to get a job and wanted me to just forget about what she had said.

"I understand that you feel like you have to say this, but I said this was going to happen in the beginning. This is what happens when you stay in someone's house, and I knew that eventually you guys would be burdened with me. My time has come, and I thank you for your kindness, but I have to man up anyway and get my shit together."

Marco still insisted that I let it go. I tried, but about a week later, things began all over again with Joanna. She came home after work ranting, and she threw the job thing out there again. I began to cry and went and bought a newspaper to look for jobs.

I called a few numbers and went around the neighborhood applying to local stores. The next day I received a phone call and was offered two jobs. I found one in Westchester, New York; it paid fifteen dollars an hour, but I would have to leave the house at four in the morning to get there. The other was working a temporary position with Verizon on Wall Street doing telemarketing for ten dollars an hour. I called a meeting with Joanna and Marco and told them that I found two jobs. Initially they were happy about it. As we discussed the details of the positions, the issue of timing—leaving and coming home—and babysitting the kids came into play. Marco didn't want me to take either of the jobs because they were too far away, and he stated that he didn't want anyone leaving his home at four in the morning while he was asleep. Marco was always paranoid like that. He didn't like it when people asked him where he was going or what he was doing when he left the house. It was kind of an unspoken rule to refrain from asking him questions.

As the conversation about the jobs continued, I slipped into a depression. Here Joanna had been telling me I needed to leave as soon as possible, and then when I found two jobs, they were telling me that I couldn't take them. I kept looking, though, and eventually found a job at a local Rite Aid. The position fit the kids' school schedule, so we were all pleased.

I worked at Rite Aid for a few months and planned to move into a room. I saved my money by giving some of my check to Joanna every time I got paid. Shortly after I began to work for Rite Aid, Joanna and Marco began to have relationship issues. Joanna thought Marco was cheating on her. So she fought with him constantly and accused him of cheating. He, of course, denied it. This was funny to me because she had been cheating on him with other guys. Then she found evidence that he was actually cheating with some chick at his job and she kicked him out of the house.

Aside from those issues, she was always getting beaten by him because he would give her thousands of dollars to pay bills, and she would blow it on Gucci bags and hanging out. I saw her get beaten many times and tried to intervene, but this infuriated him. I learned to mind my own business.

After Marco left, Joanna asked me to stay longer because she really needed my help with Marco gone. I did, and that was when I really saw what money can do for you. Joanna started talking to this guy who owned a company that was up and coming. He drove a Bentley and took us to clubs in limos. He always brought coke, and after hanging out with them a few times, I decided to do it with them. We would do coke in the clubs while drinking bottles of champagne. I began to smoke marijuana again and felt like it was okay to be doing cocaine because they were rich and they were fine doing it. Marco had been out of the house for about a month.

Here I was at seventeen hanging with grown folks in clubs like Club New York. Club New York was very popular at that time because J.Lo and P. Diddy had been involved in a shootout that had happened there. We ate at ridiculously expensive restaurants, were always in limos, and were just living life without a care in the world.

One day Marco was told by the kids that I had supported Joanna in moving on, and he came over, furious. He threatened to beat the shit out of me.

"Who the fuck do you think you are, you little faggot? Those clothes you're wearing and this house you're living in is mine. You understand me? Mine! I own this shit! You think you're going to stay here while I have to leave? Get your shit and get the fuck out!"

I packed my clothing to leave and was more nervous for

Joanna than anything else, because I was afraid she would come home with the guy she was talking to while Marco was there. Joanna eventually showed up alone while I was packing, and they began to argue. Things cooled down right around the time I finished packing.

I began to carry the garbage bag of my belongings up the stairs. Marco felt bad and asked me to stay. I wanted to so bad, but I knew my time there was up. I decided to leave but thanked them for all they did. I really had nowhere to go. The streets would have to do; after all, lacking a place to live was something I had grown accustomed to.

23

OLD
HABITS

I called Mom and told her what had happened. She said that she had bumped into an old friend named Lulu, who used to date my aunt Ava. Lulu had a room she would rent to me. I called her, and she said she was more than happy to accept me into her home. When I arrived, we discussed payment. She told me not to worry about it because I was family.

I knew that would never work beyond being a short-term arrangement, so I offered to pay her one hundred dollars a week. She accepted. Of course, I needed to support myself and pay for transportation and food. She said that the hundred dollars was more than enough. Although I had been promised a room, I gladly moved into her living room and slept on her sofa. I felt accomplished. This was the first time I worked and paid rent to support myself.

No group home, no hustling.

A FAMILIAR PATTERN

After a few weeks I began to notice that I needed to earn more than what Rite Aid had to offer. So I contacted Verizon for the position I'd found while living with Joanna and Marco and scheduled an interview. I got a job offer. I worked at Seventy-Seven Waters Place for a company that was contracted by Verizon to call its shareholders; I was paid fifteen dollars an hour. I was ecstatic! Good pay! Wow! At my age! Verizon had just become a company so the calls were to let shareholders know that the stocks were going to transfer to Verizon shares. I worked there for a while and things were looking up. A few months passed.

But this euphoria did not last. Lulu's girlfriend was released from jail. We had a new housemate. I smelled trouble when she questioned me about my rent. Oh, I knew where this was going. I answered the question, and she became frustrated.

"You think you're slick. You're working for Verizon, and I know you're making more money than you say you are. You need to start paying double or leave."

I agreed. What could I do? But that was my whole check. I was getting paid pretty well after taxes, but after food, transportation, and toiletries, I didn't have money.

Dammit, it had been going so well. But where to go? I realized that they were drug addicts. I had a flashback. Mom and Steve . . . when I was packing bags in the supermarket. I refused to let anyone else take advantage of me and my money. The drug use became more and more apparent. They looked strung out. They were crackheads and pill fiends!

They were getting high on my pay. High out of their minds. It sucked. I was sleeping on the couch, for shit's sake. And they were living the crack dream on my income. One paycheck later I came home and paid them, and the girlfriend told me that it wasn't enough. I lost it and finally defended myself.

"I am not paying you any more than I already am to sleep on a sofa! I have already doubled what I was paying before, and if you want more, I will just leave!" I was literally working to just pay them, and I was fed up. She became very aggressive and loud, threatened to kill me, and told me to leave.

I called my mother and explained what had happened. I decided to go live with Mom in the shelter system. Steve had recently been locked up again, which put her at risk of losing her room at the shelter. So the timing was perfect for the both of us.

IN LIMBO

Mom and I met up and went to the Emergency Assistance Unit (EAU), which was a homeless placement center that used to exist in the Bronx. When we arrived, we met with an assessment counselor and waited hours for a placement. The first day we weren't placed. On the nights we weren't placed, the center put us on a bus to an overnight room at around one in the morning. Just a few hours later (roughly 6 a.m.) people were rounded up into a bus and driven back to the EAU to wait again.

I was getting despondent, but anything was better than working for Lulu and her girlfriend. It took about two weeks until finally we were sent to Brooklyn HELP 1, a "tier 1" family shelter. (Tier 1 shelters were full apartments in a complex with limited visitation rights and curfew. Tier 2 shelters were independent living residences in an actual apartment building with a mix of shelter placements and regular tenants.)

During the time at the EAU, I had to call out of work a lot because we would be found ineligible for assistance if they knew I was employed. I explained the situation to my supervisor after calling out several times, and she dropped a bomb on me.

"The contract with Verizon is almost over and so we do not need your services any longer."

I was devastated! All the luxuries I had grown accustomed to faded as fast as they had come. No more Joanna and Marco, no more cash income. The reality that I was so poor was very damaging to me mentally, and I became depressed big time! I felt helpless and uneducated, and had no connections with which to turn the situation around. I also felt insecure because I could not provide for my mother the way I would have liked to. After just starting to build a good life, the walls seemed to cave in!

24

BROOKLYN HELP

When we arrived at Brooklyn Help 1, we were interviewed by a case manager and put into a unit that had a bathroom, kitchen, living room, and sleeping area. Oh, wow! We were excited to be blessed with a full apartment. Now Mom and I could set up a real home together after living apart for so many years. Just us. No Steve. No, sirree, he couldn't ruin this placement for us. The room was on the second floor, and the entire facility was in a gated community. There was one way in and one way out.

TIERS

After being there for a while, I made friends with a guy named Angelo who hung out with all of the drug dealers there. I began to hang out with them also and learned quickly how to do exactly what they were doing to survive.

With the loss of income, I did not have the luxury of choice. There was a system put into place so that there were no wars over who was selling. We (the dealers) agreed to sell whatever we wanted to our tiers. The tiers were coincidentally divided into three sections, and there were three crews. My section only sold cocaine. So I jumped on the opportunity to sell marijuana on my tier. It helped Mom and me survive.

I accompanied one of the weed dealers to his connect in downtown Brooklyn and introduced myself. I started out by purchasing an ounce of weed for about $35. I remember that drug spot like it was yesterday. If you wanted to buy drugs, you had to go to a pizza shop and talk to a guy who called the spot to give you clearance. Immediately you were escorted inside the building; the first floor was for nickels and dimes, the second floor for ounces and half ounces, and the third floor was for pounds. There were zip locks and boxes of weed everywhere. It was so nerve-wracking to walk through, thinking about the cops raiding the spot while I was there. After purchasing my half ounce, I proposed to Angelo that we sell the weed together. I would do all the funding and accounting, and he would do all the "re-up" and marketing. He accepted my offer, and from there we became partners.

This seemed a smart move. Mom supported the idea because I didn't do any of the risky stuff. All I did was bag up my weed; Angelo bought supplies and sold. I also devised a plan to make my weed bags fatter than everyone else's and offered a promo—buy four, get one free! People in the shelter loved me for this.

I considered my plan to be flawless. I had secretly been bagging up extra bags that Angelo didn't know about and sold them for one hundred percent profit. From the $35 I invested, I made about $150, of which I paid Angelo $45. In addition to the money we were making at the shelter, I began to secretly market to other people I knew outside.

I had become quite an entrepreneur. During this time I was hooking up with a guy who lived in Harlem and didn't have access to weed. When selling to him, I would jack up the price and sell him half the ounce for double what it originally cost as a whole. I also had Angelo acting as head of the shop so that if anyone from the shelter snitched, Mom and I wouldn't be evicted.

I had covered all the bases.

NO MORE DRAMA

But there was a flaw in my plan. Another Joanna! Angelo's girlfriend. She did not like me and wanted Angelo to sell on his own, to reap all the benefits. She knew he was doing all of the work and hated me for it. She poked at me every chance she had, making little comments.

"Don't worry, baby, I got my check, and you are going to work for me now. He thinks you're stupid."

She made the mistake of making a comment in front of Mom. Mom began to poke at her to let her know that she wasn't allowing anyone to mess with me. Angelo was neutral. He liked our setup and wanted to stay in it, it seemed.

One afternoon I was on our tier, and Angelo's girlfriend passed by.

"Today's the day I win this battle." she said.

I laughed. "What the fuck are you talking about? I have no problem with you. Why do you feel it necessary to fuck with me all the time?"

She smirked and walked off. Shit was about to explode. About a half hour later the phone rang. It was social services!

"Are you selling drugs? We have just received a complaint from one of the neighbors."

Mom became frustrated immediately. "We don't know what you are talking about, but I do know who said that, and I'm going to handle this bitch right now."

Mom hung the phone up and walked over to Angelo's

girlfriend. "What the fuck is your problem, bitch?"

She played dumb. "What you mean? I don't have a problem."

"Yes, you do, bitch, and it's with my son, and this shit is going to end now or I'm going to fuck you up!"

She repeated that she didn't have a problem.

"Okay, so I'm letting you know now if I hear one more comment out of your mouth or If I hear you said some shit to anyone to jeopardize our housing placement, I will fuck you up."

Joanna walked off, went downstairs, and true as hell, maybe five minutes later we received another call from social services. We had to go downstairs to the office to discuss issues that had been brought to their attention.

Shit! We were being transferred to another facility because Mom had threatened someone, and they were aware of the fact that I was selling drugs. Mom denied that we were selling drugs and pointed out that the reports were from someone who wanted to cause trouble. The social worker informed Mom that we had thirty days to leave the facility because they couldn't just ignore the reports.

Mom begged the social worker, but it was too late. She sat and thought for a few seconds and then walked out. I followed, and as we approached the tier, Mom began yelling for Joanna.

"Fuck you, bitch! I ain't going nowhere!" Joanna yelled.

In that instant, Mom lost it. She ran upstairs, walked up to Angelo's girl, and punched her in the face. She grabbed her by her hair and flung the girl over the tier down to the first floor.

Thankfully, Joanna wasn't hurt, having landed on her feet. At that point, other people wanted to get involved and security was approaching. Mom got me to pack our things, and I did so, fast. As we walked out, people asked us questions.

"What happened? Why did your mother hit her?"

"I warned that bitch to stop fucking with my son. She not only kept on fucking with him, she also got us kicked out because she's a fucking hater!"

We traveled back to the EAU for a new placement. On the

ride up Mom began to cry. It had been too much. I was numb...

"Please, Ed, no more! No more drama or bullshit. I just want to get our apartment already."

I promised her that I wouldn't get involved in selling drugs anymore. When we got to the EAU, we went through the whole process again until we were placed in a shelter in the Bronx on Stebbins Avenue.

At that point I was done dealing. And even though we were back at square one once again, I was determined to turn things around. I was ready to grow up, for real, and take control of my life.

PART THREE

EDDIE THE MAN

Mom lay there for six hours before the coroner finally arrived to remove her body. The empty, scary, hopeless feeling that enveloped my body grew every time I looked at her. Nothing I had been through could have prepared me for this moment.

25

THE BLUE ROOM

There was no apartment waiting at the Stebbins shelter. This was a tough one. Imagine, having a shared bathroom and kitchen. Our room was the size of a general living room. To add to it, we had to share only one full-size mattress! The walls were painted blue.

This was "the blue room," our new home. It was at Stebbins where Mom received her decision for the Section 8 and NYCHA application she'd submitted when she and Steve were in the shelter together. (Section 8 is a program that pays your rent either partially or in full for life, and NYCHA, or the "projects," are housing complexes that are rent stabilized for low-income people.)

It was a no! And it was based on Steve's criminal record. Steve, without batting an eyelid, had fucked it up for us. So

... no opportunity for housing for us! We felt hopeless at that point but were comforted by the fact that we had each other—and we at least had the blue room.

The reason we were placed in the room was because I was eighteen, so our family composition changed from one adult and one minor to two adults. The system categorized us as a couple who were capable of sharing a single room with a single bed.

ABBY AND VINNY

I began to apply for jobs and was called back for an interview with Petland Discounts. I aced the interview and was offered a position out in Bayside, Queens. I took the offer and worked there for the next six months. It was a two-hour ride (three buses) to and from the job, but being employed was worth it!

I can honestly say that it was one of my favorite crappy jobs ever! I love animals, so working with them was a pleasure.

Then along came Abby.

It was at this job that I learned that I was becoming a good-looking guy. There were two high schools around the area, and I used to have a little fan club of girls that came by every day. They would tell me that I was cute and try to get my number.

While I was not interested, I was flattered. My self-esteem could do with a boost.

None of them caught my eye except Abby. Abby was a fly white girl with blue eyes and a body to kill for. She was the epitome of a beautiful woman. She entered the store one day and asked for my help to buy her new dog some accessories. I offered to give her some stuff for free, and she looked at me, confused.

"I'll give you anything you need for the dog, but you have to meet me after work to pick up the stuff."

She smiled and assured me that she could pay for everything, but I insisted. She agreed to meet me. I gave her a dog collar, jacket, and a few other things. She was so grateful and shifted the conversation. Could I walk her and the dog home? I did, and as we walked, we began to make some small talk. She told me she was an administrative assistant in a hospital and lived on her own, a bus ride away from Petland. I was so nervous. I kept thinking the same thing. Why is this gorgeous woman giving me, of all people, time out of her day?

We eventually arrived at her friend's house a couple of blocks away, and she introduced me.

"This is Eddie. He is a nice guy from Petland that walked me home to make sure I got here safe."

I took a chance and asked her for her number, and she actually gave it to me. She asked that I make sure to call her, and I promised I would. I went home that night so excited and hyped up. Mom was proud that I'd finally come home with a girl's number instead of a dude's. I waited a few days before calling her.

But then along came a dude: Vinny. White . . . blue eyes. A gorgeous, masculine version of Abby. Plus he liked me, too. Vinny and I hit it off right away and began to hang out every day. He would meet me after work and we would smoke and drink and try to have sex secretly without Mom or anyone in the shelter catching us.

One time when Mom was sleeping, Vinny and I were having sex in the closet. We were trying to be quiet, but things got heavy and Mom woke up.

I heard Mom cautiously ask, "Eddie?" We shuffled to get dressed, and I thought, She is still groggy, let me mess with her.

I said in a muffled voice, "Michelle!"

"Eddie?" she responded, as though she were confused.

"Michelle, this is God speaking," I said sinisterly.

"Eddddiiiiieee?" Her voice was trembling.

We couldn't take it anymore and burst out of the closet laughing hysterically.

"Ay, stupid! You're so stupid. Don't do that, you scared

me!"

Good times!

FUCK BUDDY

Then one day at work, Abby arrived and gave me a dirty look. It was a few minutes before closing, and she wanted to buy a fish tank setup. I assisted her and tried to be sly, but she brushed me off. I asked what was wrong, and she said that she wasn't interested in me because I never called her.

I explained that I was nervous and didn't know what to say. A part of the reason I didn't call Abby was because I was embarrassed that I lived in a shelter and she made more money than I did. I didn't tell her this, but when I explained that I was nervous, she eased up and offered for me to make it up to her by spending the night in her apartment. I accepted the offer, closed the store, and headed home with her.

Her apartment made me even more insecure and nervous. It was decked out with nice furniture and very nicely put together. I set up her fish tank, and we began to make out on the sofa. My nerves eased up, and we undressed. She grabbed my penis and inserted it, and I instantly came! She was so hot and the scene was so random, that I came immediately.

"Did you come?"

"No, I didn't. That's just pre-cum. I pre-cum a lot, sorry."

I could tell she knew I was lying, but she played along. She got up and went to the bathroom. I got on the phone and called Mom.

"Mom, I don't know what to do. I think I just messed it up because I came instantly."

"Go back in and try again, papi, you can do it." Mom was great about these matters. I hung up, and Abby returned to the bed. We continued to make out, and this time when I got inside, I came in about thirty seconds. This time it seemed okay.

"If you came, it's okay. I understand."

I admitted that I did, and we just hung out and watched TV.

The next morning Abby and I went to take the bus to go to work, and I asked if we could chill again.

"I like you and want to get to know you more."

"All I want is a fuck buddy and that's it. I'm not looking for a relationship."

I felt shut down. "Okay."

HONESTLY

At work, my manager Rey was so proud of me because he loved Abby. I gave him all the details. He broke the news that he wanted to promote me to assistant manager! I accepted, and he said that I needed to take a drug test. I admitted to him that I smoked marijuana. I had to get clean for the test, he said. So I did, and when I went for the testing, I passed. But during a post-test interview with the investigator, I admitted that I had a history of marijuana use but had stopped using for the job. I didn't know that I demolished any chance of getting the position by being honest.

When I went to work the next day, they were pissed at me and informed me that the district manager didn't want to promote me based on the answers I had given about my history.

Again, honesty fucked things up for me! I was so disappointed and lost interest in the job. I began to sell products to local regulars on the side to make money. I knew it was just a matter of time before they fired me, so I needed to save up.

NONE

Things with Vinny were picking up, and he told me he loved me. I began to take him seriously and started a relationship with him. Two months later Abby began to look for me. I received word from her friends that she wanted to talk to me, but I avoided her. One night around 3 a.m., while lying in bed with Vinny, I received a phone call from Abby. I answered my cell phone half asleep.

"Hello?"

"What the hell is wrong with you?!"

I was confused and asked what the hell she was talking about.

"Do you know who the hell I am? I could have any guy I want! Why don't you want me?"

"Didn't you say you didn't want anything serious?"

"Of course I want to be with you," she said. I thought for a second, and the reality that she knew nothing about me being poor or bisexual or that I had Vinny lying next to me popped into my head. I told her I was sorry, but I had begun to date someone else.

She demanded that I meet her right then. I said I was sorry, but I couldn't. She hung up on me, and that was the last I heard of her. I'll admit that if Vinny were not there, I would have met up with her, because I was seriously into this girl. But it would have looked really bad to get up at 3 a.m. and leave him there, so I didn't.

A week or so later, I went through Vinny's cell phone and saw that he was texting other men and hooking up with them. A combination of frustration, disappointment, and foolishness would best describe how I felt. I approached him, and he got mad and broke up with me. I was devastated.

So no Abby, and no Vinny!

When I tried to call Abby back, her phone was disconnected. I lost both of them in the same week and was an emotional wreck!

BACK IN THE SYSTEM

Kira came to stay with Mom and me at the shelter on occasion because my aunt had kicked her out to go stay with my uncle Hector, like she'd done with me. Mom and I were called into a meeting with the social workers one day, and we were evicted.

They evicted us because we had too many visitors in and out of the room.

Once again, Mom and I went back to EAU and through the whole placement process. During the process we couldn't leave the building at any time or we would lose our placement, so I wasn't able to go to work without risking being put out into the streets. I called Rey and explained the issue. Rey told me that he could excuse me for two days, but after that I would have to be terminated.

Of course we weren't placed for an entire week, so I was fired. I was a wreck when I lost my job. I had lost Vinny, Abby, and my income. Life started to suck again for what seemed like forever.

26

MY WORST FEAR

Initially the Parkview shelter seemed horrible! Double the drug abuse, gang activity, and violence we had encountered in all the other shelters. But with time, we got used to it and made the best of it. Unlike the previous placements, Mom and I were given separate rooms. We still shared a bathroom and kitchen with everyone on the floor. The rooms were closet sized, but we were happy to have somewhere to live once again.

THE FAVOR

During this period my dad was released from prison and came back into our lives. At first Kira and I were excited that he was back, but we hadn't the slightest clue as to the kind of father he would actually be.

Dad was always working his construction job. When we hung out with him, he spent the time telling us that we amounted to nothing and needed to get our acts together. His exact words: "You guys are fucking bums. Get your shit together and do what the fuck you have to do."

He insisted that Kira and I get our GEDs and good jobs because he wouldn't want anything to do with us otherwise. The energy in the room was always awkward. We thought he was an asshole for it but signed up for a GED class and looked for jobs.

Dad was always a ladies' man. A few months after his release, he'd met a woman who was married to a white man and had a son. She lived out in New Jersey and met him during a blackout while walking uptown from work. In order for them to have sex, he would have to bring her test results showing an HIV negative status. Dad and I were talking about her one day and he asked me to go get tested for HIV. He said that he wanted me to test under his name so that he could get my result to take to her because he was too busy with work and had no time to get tested himself. I found this odd but agreed to do him the favor. I was excited that I could do my dad a favor and help him out, maybe score some cool son points.

THE DIAGNOSIS

For weeks prior to my father asking me to do this, I had told Mom and Kira that I felt different. I didn't know what it was, but I just knew something about me felt different. Mom and Kira kept telling me I was nuts and nothing was wrong with me, but I knew something was up. I even went as far as saying that I was scared because I thought it might be the worst thing of all. I had been feeling tired and weak. Every time I mentioned that I wasn't feeling well and was worried that something was wrong with me, Mom and Kira looked scared and told me to stop worrying.

Across the street from the shelter was this little private clinic, so I decided to go in. I scheduled a complete physical. While in the waiting area, I ate two Snickers bars, drank a soda, and had some potato chips. I was called in and had my physical done. I requested the HIV test, and the doctor explained that if I wanted that specific test done then I would need to go to a separate lab to have blood drawn. So I left his office and traveled to a LabCorp where I was tested for HIV.

PAUSE

About two weeks later, I returned to the doctor's office for my results. All my labs were fine except for my blood sugar level. He explained that it was extremely high, that he thought I might be a diabetic, and he needed to have me tested further. I was given an appointment to return for a diabetes follow-up for three weeks later.

During the waiting period, I hung out with Kira a bit, who at the time was dating a lesbian. Our conversation somehow shifted to HIV. When the subject came up, I said that I had recently been tested and my results were good. Kira's girlfriend said that she recently tested also and pulled out a letter from the Department of Health that confirmed her negative status. I read the letter and congratulated her. My immediate reaction was, "I didn't get one!"

She looked at me and raised her eyebrows. "Well, you only get one if you're negative."

I made a mental note to request my letter to give to Dad. It was nerve-wracking waiting to go back for the diabetes follow-up. During that time frame, coincidently, I must've seen about ten commercials raising HIV awareness. I saw countless "Get tested and know your results" billboards and was even approached by a few random local outreach workers and given condoms.

The day of the appointment finally arrived. While waiting to meet with the doctor, my stomach turned. I felt like I was about to find out something really bad but comforted myself with the fact the doctor would've said something if the results were abnormal. When I was called in to meet with the doctor, I immediately requested the letter verifying my negative status. The doctor looked at my file and said that I hadn't been tested for HIV.

I explained that I did get the test at the lab. He asked the secretary to contact the lab to have them fax the results over. He stated that I needed to be tested for diabetes to identify what type I had. While we were discussing diabetes, the fax came through. I became even more nervous at this point because the secretary looked at the results and then immediately looked up at me with concern.

My heart was pounding. I was getting paranoid and needed to relax. The doctor asked me to wait outside for a moment while he made a phone call. I was called in, and the doctor looked at me and said, "Your results came back positive." He was blunt!

The room swirled in slow motion.

"What?" My voice was disassociated from me. Whose voice was this?

He repeated it.

"There's no way."

He looked at me. "How do you feel?"

"What am I supposed to feel? I'm going to die!"

Tears began to run down my face . . . again, as if it was not a part of me.

"Well, I'm sorry, and you need to talk to the secretary, who will schedule you an appointment with an infectious disease clinic."

I numbly walked out. Eddie the robot took over and asked the secretary for an appointment. She gave me a list of infectious disease clinics and told me to call any one of them myself.

I was going to die. What should I do? Who should I tell? Should I stay quiet and not say anything and just die? How long do I have?

There were many more questions racing through my head during the walk home. At home I curled into a fetal position and just cried. After about thirty minutes, the first person I thought to call was my stepmother Joanna. Mom was at her methadone maintenance program, so I didn't have any way to contact her. I called Joanna, crying.

"Eddie, what's wrong."

"I'm scared, Joanna. Got bad news."

"Oh, my God, Eddie. Please don't tell me what I think you're going to tell me."

"I'm HIV positive, J."

She broke down and started crying with me. I thought about refraining from telling more people for fear of rejection, or being stigmatized or viewed as a statistic.

When Mom arrived home and saw my face, she knew it was big. I told her what had happened, and she broke down crying. She asked if they were sure, and I told her they referred me to an infectious disease clinic. Mom hugged me and then she kind of stared, way off into the distance. It still felt like Eddie the robot was going through the motions.

I could tell she was concerned and feared exactly what I did, that I was going to die. Kira randomly popped by that night to hang out, and I told her. She cried, too. I could see the look . . . almost like disappointment. This was something a few people had considered to be a possibility because I was gay, but they'd never expected it to actually happen.

Nor did I. Not only was I positive, but I had predicted that I was, without really thinking so or having any reason to feel that way—except that I knew my body and something wasn't right.

A few days later, I found the balls to call my father and tell him. I called him, hysterically crying.

"Eddie, what's wrong . . ."

"I'm sorry, Dad, but I can't give you the results you need because I'm positive." I felt stupid and like I let him down. I couldn't provide the results he needed.

"Wow, bro, are you sure? You need to relax."

I kept crying and told him I was sure. About a minute in he says . . .

"Yo. I don't have time for this right now because you caught me in the middle of something. I'll call you in a few. Or you can call me when you calm down. You're going to be fine. Crying isn't going to solve anything, so stop the emotional bullshit."

Say what? My dad was blowing me off, like it was nothing. Was this some tough love shit? For the next few weeks, my view on life was so different. All I could think about was when I was going to die. I feared going to hell and wondered if my status was punishment from God for being homosexual.

There was so much bullshit about it being a punishment at the time. My mind just wandered aimlessly into deep thoughts that I hadn't ever had before. As each day would pass, I wondered if it were my last.

HOPE RETURNS

A few weeks after my diagnosis, I got a random visit from some guy who said that he worked for the outreach department with an organization called Harlem United. He said that they would help me with food and transportation if I gave him some of my time. I was more than interested because of the Metro cards and food he offered. He explained to me that he knew I was newly diagnosed and that there were services I was entitled to based on my status. He said that I could get an apartment, increased public assistance amounts, and free comprehensive medical care.

I didn't believe him. He kept promising me that he would work on it. It was during that session with the outreach worker that I regained a sense of hope. We spent over an hour discussing how HIV treatment had progressed and how it was no longer a death sentence because of new medications. I began to feel alive again.

A month later I spoke with Dad on the phone. He wanted to know what I had done about my health since getting the results. I explained that I was told to call an infectious disease clinic to make an appointment but didn't want to. (I guess I didn't follow up because I was still in denial. I never thought I would become HIV positive. I had always prided myself on being somewhat educated on the topic. I actually believed I was one of the lucky people who couldn't be affected by the virus.)

My dad told me that we were going to take a day and go to the hospital together to address the issue. Quite a surprise after his nonchalance. We met and walked into New York Presbyterian Hospital's emergency room. I said, "I just found out that I'm HIV positive and want to speak to someone who knows what I should do." We waited a while in the pediatrics waiting room and eventually spoke with a doctor who said that NYP had a great clinic. The doctor scheduled an appointment for a confirmatory test and medical follow-up.

When I returned for my appointment, I was, of course, hopeful that the confirmatory test would be negative and release me. I was given a Western blot test, which is the most accurate—the results were still positive.

I met with my doctor, Joseph Stavola. He and I spent the next hour addressing every question I had. He was the best. After six months of working with Dr. Stavola, I went from planning my funeral to planning my life.

"You're going to outlive me, kid," he told me during that first meeting. "You have more chances of getting hit by a bus than dying from this virus so long as you take your medications every day on time."

This was huge. It renewed my hope, and I dedicated myself to becoming educated about HIV. I had the option to start a drug regimen right away or wait till my viral load increased to a point where medications were absolutely necessary. I decided to begin medications immediately, out of fear, and within a month or so, my status changed to "undetectable." In the world of HIV, being "undetectable" is when you have a very low amount of the virus in your blood.

It was the best result I could have hoped for. That said, taking the medications in the beginning was a challenge in itself. I had to get used to taking a pill twice a day when I never had to take medication in my life. The medications made me very nauseous, and I threw up regularly for the first few weeks.

MORE PROGRESS

During my time at Parkview Shelter I had befriended someone who worked for Cosi, a sandwich/coffee shop. He promised that he would try to hook me up with a job there as a barista. I aced the interview and was hired. I was so happy to be employed again that I did everything in my power to keep the job. I didn't steal from them and really worked hard. I excelled as a barista and was given a few raises.

It was at that job where I met Jody. Jody was this hot Dominican woman that every guy wanted and I thought I could never have. After working the night shift together and conversing a few times, Jody and I began to date. She was a sweet girl and had a killer body. I remember asking her out, and when she accepted, I felt like the man.

Things were beginning to pick up for me. Not only did I find a job and a hot girlfriend, but the guy from Harlem United came through on his promise and found a program that could help us obtain housing.

Mom and I were called over to meet with the Harlem United–Women and Children's program director. This program housed HIV-infected or -affected women and their children. The director was a nice Caucasian woman who empathized with our situation. She listened to our background as she did an assessment. She explained that HASA was a section of public assistance that pays 100 percent rent if the person infected with HIV meets their criteria. She also explained that medical information needed to be requested from my doctor in order to determine eligibility. I signed some paperwork, and at my next appointment, I explained everything to Dr. Stavola.

He was very familiar with our situation because it was all I spoke about in our sessions. He hooked me up and provided the documentation to make me eligible for HASA. Within three weeks I was accepted to receive HASA, and Mom and I had appointments to look at the two-bedroom apartments they had available. The first apartment we saw, we took. We were so desperate to be housed—we had been homeless for so long—that we didn't want to waste time being picky. Within a month of accepting the apartment, we moved in.

RIP DOC

Almost five years to the day after my original meeting with Dr. Stavola, I was listening to the news and heard that a Dr. Joseph Stavola had been killed by a fallen tree while on vacation. He had been driving when a tree struck his car. He and his wife were killed, but their two children survived. I'd never cried for anyone who'd died before this, but this news floored me, and I felt as though my sense of security with my status had been shaken as well. The hairs on my arm raised, and I got the chills.

I mean, I randomly tune in to the news, and this is what I hear? Was this his way of saying, "I told you you would outlive me, kid," from the afterlife?

Rest in peace, Dr. Stavola.

27

RELATIONSHIPS

As my **health and home** life stabilized, I could move on with my love life. Telling my partners about my status was difficult, though it would turn out be something that brought me to my first long-term relationship.

JODY

Jody and I dated for a few months. She was very seductive and sexually in tune—to say the least. The first time we hung out, she wanted to have sex. I didn't want to, though, because I feared having to tell her that I was positive. It hung like a cloud between us.

I remember that night like it was yesterday. We were making out, and she asked me to have sex with her. I went to look for a condom and realized that we didn't have any.

"Wait, I have to go get a condom."

She grabbed me, looked me in my eyes, and begged for me to go in without a condom. This was playing with fire! I was tempted to but didn't want to do that to her. I tried to leave, but she didn't give in. She wanted it right then and there. We were naked. Temptation was like a red hot chili! I didn't give in, though, and I went to the store to get a condom. She was pissed.

When I came back, she still seemed mad, but we got back to business straight away. The next morning we were sitting in my room, and she said that the night before was a hot experience. I agreed, and as we spoke, she asked the question I'd been dreading.

"Why didn't you just fuck me without a condom last night? Do you have a disease or something?"

I looked at her and paused for a moment. This was it. Any other time I could say no. It was quiet. So quiet. I became overwhelmed with emotion and broke down crying. I had never done this before! I couldn't control my emotions. I had to express to someone that I was HIV positive. And it was a partner. A girlfriend. She looked at me, confused. I looked at her.

"I'm sorry, but I do. I'm HIV positive," I said, and I just kept crying like a baby.

She looked shocked. She hugged me and thanked me for sharing and protecting her from becoming infected.

From that moment on I felt like I needed to tell her everything. If she was to be my wife or long-term girlfriend, I couldn't hide that I was bisexual from her. I used Mom and my friend Marquis to break the news to her. One night while hanging out, Marquis put himself out there and told her he was gay. She was taken aback. It did not go down well. I was discouraged. But this was the moment of truth.

Maybe a week or so later, I told her that I had one more secret. She looked at me, worried. I said I was bisexual, and she laughed out loud. She didn't believe me. I continued to try

to convince her for the next two days until she ‚
it. She said that she was having a hard time gr
secrets, but she would stay with me no matte
this was it. I finally got her where I needed her ᴜ
going to be my first long-term relationship.

But, sadly, I soon found out she was still talking to her ex,
the guy she'd supposedly left to be with me. When I found out,
I cut her off immediately. I wanted to be with her but wasn't
ready to deal with cheating and other men. After all, I had just
moved into my first apartment, and was finally breaking out of
depression after my diagnosis.

I began to date men again. Women were complex. I was
tired of women and their confusing ways of dealing with relationships. Mostly, men were always very clear as to what their
intentions were.

SCANDY

Getting back into men was simple. I called the New York Donut
(chat line) and began listening to ads describing guys. There
was a tanned Puerto Rican guy who was looking to hook up.
We spoke and planned to meet. The day we met, he came to
my apartment, and when I greeted him at the door, I knew he
was something more than just a hook up. I thought he was
amazingly cute. Tanned, with a full goatee, Scandy was actually quite masculine. We chatted, breaking the ice. The doorbell rang.

It was Mom with a surprise twist. She'd brought my lit-
tle brother Robert and sisters Marisa and Tamara with her!
I was so happy because I hadn't seen them for almost a year.
I got so caught up in catching up with Marisa, Robert, and
Tamara that I forgot Scandy was in my room waiting for me.
He must've been in my room for a half hour before I realized
that he was still there. I apologized to him and explained that
I hadn't seen my siblings for some time. He was understanding
and waited for me to finish.

When I finished catching up with them, I spent the rest of the night talking to Scandy. We had so many things in common that we forgot we were hooking up and didn't have sex that night. Scandy went to work the next day, and when he got out, we met up at my house again. He must've spent the night every night for the next three weeks.

Almost a month later, Scandy and I finally wanted to have sex. We had flirted and made out a lot before but never took it to the next level. Before we did, I hesitated, but I told him my status. He looked at me with a blank expression. He looked down.

"Oh, my God, you're positive. So am I!" Then he began to cry.

This explained why we had both waited, flirted, and gotten to know each other cautiously.

I was shocked. It reminded me of telling Jody. He had been diagnosed a year ago but hadn't been to the doctor since. The poor guy was waiting to die and had that perception of the virus that I'd had when I was first diagnosed. He hadn't even told his family that he was positive. I explained to him the array of services available to people with HIV and stressed the importance of a good support system.

That night I made him call his mother and tell her what she needed to know. After he finished breaking down with his mother on the phone, I told him that he needed to go to the doctor with me to be connected to care. He agreed to go and was eventually connected to my clinic where he began receiving care with me. Things were looking up for us . . . but there was more.

28

EDDIE THE ADVOCATE

Whenever I went to a clinic appointment, I would see a social worker. I made it a point to stress my employment needs because the income I had from Cosi wasn't making ends meet. My social worker gave me a flyer that asked for young men who have sex with men to apply to become peer educators. It paid ten bucks an hour and was an opportunity to be trained in nonprofit HIV education work.

A NEW PURPOSE

After interviewing with Serette King, a representative of People of Color in Crisis, I was hired. I received training in HIV 101, STDs, prevention, harm reduction, and outreach. I even went out to the Center for Disease Control (CDC) in Atlanta to assist in advocating for more funding for youth services. The trip was all expenses paid; I had my own hotel room in a four-star hotel and was flown out to Atlanta.

I loved this job. It was all gay men of color running an organization funded by the CDC. There were so many things I learned there. I learned a lot about gay culture. Prior to this experience I had never known about the ball scene, voguing competitions, and gay lingo.

I worked for People of Color in Crisis for two years, until the funding for our contract was exhausted.

A TRUE CALLING

I submitted an entry essay for an internship at an organization called Public Allies. It promised to pay $4,725 for college upon completion and paid $1,700 a month for ten months in the program. In addition, I could continue to receive public assistance because the money I received fell under some law where public assistance couldn't use the income to cut me off. I was accepted, after which I interviewed with six partner organizations. I was matched with Palladia as a community follow-up worker who would provide case management support to HIV-positive families and conduct outreach to bring in new clients.

I loved this position and the Public Allies experience. I was taken on three retreats, trained on coalition building, and was a part of a team service project aimed at creating structural changes. I met many different people and acquired more professional skills during my ten months there. Upon completion of the Public Allies experience, I did a "presentation of learning" as part of my requirements to finish the program. The Senior Director of Centralized Admissions for Palladia, Zoleka Adams, attended my presentation to be of support.

I had grown so much, and had become empowered. My self-esteem had grown, together with my knowledge of living with HIV, creating support programs, and implementing structural changes. Eddie the frightened child had come a long way.

I poured my heart out in that presentation. I spoke about the life I had lived up until joining Public Allies, and the new perspective I'd gained.

After the presentation, Zoleka Adams made an announcement. She said she was proud of me and was happy to say that I would always have a position at Palladia. From that moment on I was employed full-time as a Community Follow-up Worker. Within months I was promoted to Admissions Counselor for Palladia's drug treatment programs where I did assessments to determine a client's eligibility for drug treatment. The things I have heard and seen while servicing the community are confidential, so I am not at liberty to discuss them, but they have humbled me and, at times, made me cry. So many people have had fucked-up lives and became victims of their situations, just like I did.

A REAL HOME

Back at home, things were great. Scandy had moved in with me, and Kira began to stay there as well. Although Mom was still living with us, she was also still sucked into Steve's warped sense of reality and made sure to visit him in prison every chance she got. And she continued to give him her Social Security check while he was in prison. That's how much of a hold Steve had on her. This annoyed the hell out of me because I felt like I had finally provided a safe space for us, and she still wanted to be with Steve. We argued whenever Steve was mentioned because I refused to accept that she was supporting his habits in prison, while we were trying to survive.

I always wanted the best for Mom. Why did she not want it for herself? Mom always argued that she needed to deal with him in order to see her children. Steve's mother, Selma, had custody of the kids at that time, and Steve used that as leverage against Mom. He would tell her that if she didn't give him money then he wouldn't advocate for his mother to let her see them. Steve's mother was always a bitch to us for no reason.

She had this vendetta with my mother that never ended. I always argued that Mom should clean up completely and go to court to fight for her rights. (After we had been removed by ACS, her parental rights were terminated.) She felt that that was too much of a task and would rather deal with Steve.

As the kids grew older, Selma's hold on them grew weaker. They began to call Mom and play hooky from school to have visits with her, like I did when I was their age. When Robert and Marisa reached ages thirteen and fourteen, Selma decided to give them up. I went to court and filed a petition for custody of the two because I felt that I could provide a loving home for them. It was the perfect opportunity to reunite with my siblings after being separated for so long.

My life was on track. I could give them so much more than random and group homes. A real family home.

FAMILY COURT

The court process was gruesome. Selma and Steve's sister, Cindy, who also didn't like us, went into court guns blazing. They hired an attorney, when all I had was a free Legal Aid representative. They insisted that I was a drug addict "just like my mother." That I was "gay" and "sick." Of course none of these things except the drug use held any weight in court.

Luckily, I had anticipated them putting all of my dirty laundry out to air, so I made sure to quit smoking marijuana long before petitioning. I was drug tested, my home was inspected, and after a few short months, I was awarded temporary custody of Robert and Marisa.

This was a big achievement.

Selma kept custody of Sara and Tamara. It was then that she decided to place them in a boarding school to get rid of the responsibility and really stick it to Mom. She did not want them. But neither could Mom have them.

If they were three hours away with people who were instructed not to let them have any communication with us, then how could we see them? Or at least that's what she thought. I took care of that by asking the courts for visitation rights. The courts instructed me to keep them all away from Mom, and I agreed, but I let Mom have all the time she wanted.

Mom never harmed any of us. She loved us more than she valued her own life. There were so many times that ACS came to visit, and I had to hide Mom in the closet or have her climb out of a window so that ACS wouldn't remove the kids.

I was holding us all together. I began to feel a sense of accomplishment. I thought I was the man. Nothing could break me down.

I'd finally grown up, secured an apartment and a job I loved, and reunited as many of us as I could.

Life was good. At last.

29

WHEN TIME STOPPED

The signs were everywhere. We were blind to them. For an entire month, Mom kept telling me that she was having this dream of God asking her to come and fight his final battle with him. She said that she kept saying, "But I can't leave my kids behind."

"Have faith—Eddie will take care of them." This was God's reply.

"If something was to ever happen to me, will you make sure the kids are okay?" she'd ask me.

"Of course, Mom."

"Really, Ed? That is a lot. Are you sure?"

"Of course, Mom, but stop talking like that. Nothing is going to happen to you if you take care of yourself."

Mom came home one day and said that the doctor found

something wrong with her heart. I asked what they thought it might be, and she said they didn't know but she had an appointment scheduled for a follow-up to determine the actual issue. I did what I had been accustomed to doing, which was to blame it on the countless cigarettes she smoked daily, her lack of healthy choices, and drug use.

A TOUGH DISCUSSION

Whenever we encountered an issue around the kids, Mom and I would conference about it together. This particular conversation revolved around the issue of school: Marisa was failing half her classes, and Robert was beginning to drop in his grades. I was frustrated, so Scandy, Mom, and I discussed the issue.

I had so easily slipped into the role of home- and decision-maker. I felt like I'd laid down the rules, and they knew what was expected of them. I wanted to discipline them. Mom was defending them, and as I argued with her about the issue, all of a sudden, she grabbed her chest. She was in pain.

"Are you okay?"

"I am okay." But she wasn't. Scandy looked genuinely concerned. Regrettably, I thought she was trying to deflect, to distract me from the subject at hand.

"Whatever. You're just covering for them, and they're getting out of control. If you don't find a way to handle them, I will."

She tried to reassure me that she really had a pain, that she understood, and that she agreed with me. I wasn't hearing it.

A SENSE OF PEACE

It was during this time that I had begun to seek a larger apartment to accommodate all of us, including the children. I had recently viewed a large, beautiful, three-bedroom apartment and begun the paperwork process with HASA to transition. I fell in love with this apartment immediately. It was fully carpeted, had two bathrooms (one in the master bedroom), a large living room, and great amenities like a dishwasher and huge closet space. I remember seeing Mom that day when she got home.

I ran up to her. "Mom, I have great news!"

"I have great news, too, papi. You go first."

I informed her about the apartment.

"That's great, and I have even better news for you. You know the whole God and homosexuality thing that we've spoken about? Well, after doing some research and speaking to a few religious people, I have concluded that you aren't going to hell! The same rules apply to gay people as they do to straight people. As long as you are faithful and stay with one partner, you can be saved! Isn't that great?"

In that moment I felt like my mother had finally found peace with my sexuality. She had always been supportive but had concerns in terms of where I was with God. My mother loved me unconditionally—I, too, finally felt a sense of peace with who I was, after worrying about my afterlife for so many years. Until that moment, I'd thought I was going to hell simply because I was who I was.

In the excitement, Mom's health concerns were temporarily forgotten. We were caught up in the issues with kids and our preparations to move into our new apartment, and Mom never mentioned having chest pains to me and Scandy again.

ONE LAST PARTY

On December 1, 2006, Mom received her SSI check and came to me.

"This is it, Eddie. I am giving you my entire check for you to budget for me for the month. All I ask is that you budget my hair, nails, and a pair of Timberlands for my birthday."

Mom's birthday was December 19. I was so proud of her.

Finally, after years of arguing and fighting over the issue of her SSI check, she used it for herself, not for Steve. I felt like things were finally in a good place and my dream of putting us all in a house without Steve was becoming a reality.

That night, Scandy and I planned to go to No Parking, a gay bar in Washington Heights. We had been together almost a year and a half by then. Occasionally, we had threesomes with other guys or foursomes with other couples to keep our relationship interesting. We acknowledged that we were both young and didn't want to ruin a great relationship by doing things with other people behind each other's backs.

Mom asked that I drive her to Manhattan to pick up some cocaine so she could relax at the house by herself while we went out to the club. I had borrowed Kira's girlfriend's car that day—but was not permitted to drive at the time.

"I'll take you, but I can't bring you back, because if I get pulled over, they are going to see that I don't have a license, and you're going to have coke on you. So we would all go to jail if I did."

She was okay with that, and I drove her downtown to Pops' building. I continued with my day, buying clothing for the club and getting ready to go out. She returned home and offered me some blow, which I turned down.

"Damn, Ed. I bought a lot of coke. You sure you don't want some? This is a lot for me to do alone."

"Nah, Mom, I don't want any. I don't want to do that anymore."

"Okay. More for me. I'll just hold on to it for later on in the week so I can have some to chill."

Before we left for the club that night, I asked Mom to clean up the apartment a little bit because if we found a guy to bring home, we didn't want to bring him to a dirty place. Mom had no problem with cleaning up for me.

THE CALL

We went to the club and had a blast. Around three in the morning, I received a phone call from Mom.

"Papito, I just wanted to call you and let you know that the apartment is clean and you can be comfortable with bringing someone over."

I thanked her.

"I love you, papito. Have fun and be safe. I'll see you when you get home."

Scandy and I had gone out with our friend Marquis, and while at the club, we had run into two of his friends, who we wound up bringing to the house to finish off the night. When we got there, Mom greeted us in the living room. I noticed that she was looking a little weird, but I paid it no mind because I thought maybe her medications had kicked in. The medications she was on (methadone and psych meds) made her appear as though she were under the influence of (illegal) drugs.

She had a Heineken in her hand and had offered us a drink from a six pack. Mom rarely drank, so I didn't think anything of it. She sat down with us in the living room, and we got into conversation. The two guys that came over liked Mom a lot. We spoke about sex, and the two guys were going off about how cool my mom was.

"I wish I had a mom like her. She's cool, yo."

I was used to these comments. Mom was great.

About a half hour into hanging out, Mom began to slur her words, and I got a little embarrassed and pulled her into her room. We closed the door.

"Mom, it's time for you to go to bed."

"Okay, papi. Can you help me take off my sneakers?"

I did.

"Can you put them on the window so they can air out?"

I laughed. "Damn, Mom, that's ghetto that you have to put your shits in the window to prevent overload of funk."

She laughed and slurred something I didn't understand.

"Mom, I really want you to start taking care of yourself

because you're only getting older and the kids are depending on you to be there for them."

"You know what, spaghetti Eddie, this is the first time in years I've really felt like you love me like you used to love me, and I love you for that. I promise I'm going to start to change."

"All right, Mom. I love you and good night."

"I love you, too. Good night, papi."

I left her in her room to go to sleep. I rejoined the guys. After talking for a few minutes, I went to sleep.

TIME STOPS

I woke up the next morning around 11 a.m. to pee. I walked over to the bathroom and before I started to pee, I thought, I should check on Mom.

I just walked over to her room. The door was locked. I looked in the living room; one of the guys was still sleeping, but Marquis and the other guy had left for work.

That's strange, why would she lock the door? I ignored it and walked to the bathroom to pee again, but again I thought, No. I have to check on her.

I knocked really hard. There was no answer.

"Mom!" Nothing. I went to the kitchen and grabbed a butter knife. I used it to unlock the door, and there she was, lying face down on the bed with her feet hanging off the side.

She's sleeping, I told myself.

"Mom, wake up." Louder. No response. I came over to her side and pushed her back and forth.

"Mom, wake up. Mom." Nothing. She's just in a deep sleep. I kept tugging at her and instinctively, I turned her over. I pushed her sideways and saw her face—lifeless.

Instantly, my heart dropped! I knew that she was dead.

I am bugging out. She is fine. Again I felt like a robot, mechanically calling, "Mom, Mom." Like the day I heard I was positive, I was doing everything automatically.

I shook her. Nothing. There was mucous running from her

nose. I looked down. She had urinated on herself.

Mom was gone. My mother was dead. I still was in denial. I called her and called her until I lifted one of her eyelids to see that her eyes had no life in them at all. My world at that moment paused, and I realized that my mother was gone forever. I called Scandy into the room.

"Scandy, call an ambulance. I think Mommy's dead." I was calm.

"What?!"

He rushed into the room and began to panic, calling 911 frantically. Meanwhile the guy on the sofa woke up because he heard what was going on. He became frantic, too.

"Get her on the floor so I can try CPR," he said.

We did, and he pumped her chest and tried to blow life into her lifeless body. It was too late.

I broke. I cried, screamed, and cried. Then I called Kira.

"Mom is dead, Kira!"

"What?! Stop playing with me!"

I explained what had happened, and she jumped in a cab to come over. I called my aunt Ava, Selma, Pops, and the kids. It was over.

My rock. My support. My teacher. My best friend. My partner in crime.

My MOTHER had died.

She lay there on the floor, lifeless, while we cried on her. Kira came in, and she broke down. She screamed frantically and begged Mom to come back. Kira apologized to her over and over while she begged, "Please, Mommy, come back. Please!"

I literally had to peel her off Mom. A few minutes later my father arrived with his girlfriend. I was comforted by his presence for just a moment until he looked at Kira, grabbed her stomach, and told her she had gained weight. Immediately, I was turned off. I thought, "My mother is lying there on the floor dead and that's the only thing that comes out of your mouth?" Again, I was reminded of his insensitivity, like when I called to say I was positive.

My aunt Ava arrived with family members and friends, and they all broke down. Mom lay there for six hours before the coroner finally arrived to remove her body. During this time the empty, scary, hopeless feeling that enveloped my body grew every time I looked at her. Nothing I had been through could have prepared me for this moment. The way I felt the day I was diagnosed with HIV, all of the beatings, abuse, and pain prior didn't even come close to how I felt when I lost my mother.

Mom, I love you. Rest in peace.

30

THE
FUNERAL

Mom was gone. I had to deal with it. It was a first for me. How does one plan a funeral? How do you bury the woman you loved all your life?

Aunt Ava helped me. She located Francisco Funeraria, a funeral home on 115th Street and 1st Avenue in Manhattan. I was both horrified and excited at the thought of the funeral: I would be able to see my mother again. Even though she was dead, at least I would get to see her one more time in the flesh. I can remember the anticipation. It was just two days after her death, and it felt like I hadn't seen her in years.

Then the day dawned. I hopped into a cab and headed to the funeral early to be the first one there. During the cab ride, I cried my eyes out. The cab driver, a woman, asked what was wrong.

"Nothing."

She looked at me in the mirror. "Don't worry about it, pa. God is with you, and he'll make sure everything is okay."

In that instant I felt Mom's presence. My hairs stood up. All I could think of was Mom's dream and that God would make sure everything was okay. I thanked the woman for her kind words. Then we arrived.

Just looking at the funeral home was chilling. Then I approached Mom's casket. This was it! I broke down again when I saw her. The room was empty, and she lay there alone, waiting, in her white casket. I cried to Mom, for Mom, for all the years we had spent together, and for those when I longed to be with her. I cried because I could not say goodbye.

About a half hour later, everyone arrived. Everyone except Steve. Steve was in jail. Even Diane Sawyer came by and paid her respects. Callie, my sister who was removed from my mother as a baby, was there. That was the first time in almost fifteen years she'd seen Mom or any of us.

Since this was my first funeral, I did things a little differently. I took pictures with Mom and all her kids. I made a little speech about Mom and the type of person she was. Everyone was there. All seven of her children. All with Mom. I was overcome!

I attached an iPod to some speakers and played 80s freestyle, which was Mom's favorite genre of music. She had been asking me to make her a freestyle CD for a few weeks. Marisa sang Christina Aguilera's "Hurt" for Mom, and Scandy sang, too. I had used Mom's SSI money—the check she'd given me the day before she died—to buy her flowers for her casket. I asked Titi Ava to buy her the Timberlands she wanted so she could at least wear them for her funeral. I couldn't afford to pay for the funeral, so we gathered money from family and friends.

The next day we took the casket to Rosemount Cemetery in New Jersey to have Mom buried. I wanted her to be local in New York, but due to money issues, we were just grateful that we were able to pull enough money together to have a funeral and burial. Each one of us kids carved a message into Mom's casket before they put her into the ground.

As we left, I felt empty. Everyone was here. But there was no one. No Mom. Gone forever.

The next few days were pensive for me. All I could think of was what Mom stood for and taught us throughout all the trauma we had experienced. She was insightful. And at the end she prepared us for her death. She always read the bible, and she loved God above all. Mom was the most cool, down-to-earth, around-the-way kind of person—one who would smoke a blunt with you while quoting the bible front to back. As dysfunctional as that may sound, she was actually the most loving, giving, caring, and harmless person I've ever met.

She always stressed to all her children that we "should have faith in God no matter what." She'd say that he was watching our every move and would make sure that we were okay come hell or high water.

The night of the burial, Tamara spent the night in my apartment. At bedtime Scandy and I were in Mom's bedroom getting ready to sleep. Tamara came to the door and asked if she could come in. What do I say to her? What would Mom say?

In that moment I remembered that a few weeks prior Mom had told me that Tamara was still very young minded and needed to be treated like a baby (holding her in your arms and putting her to sleep and things like that). I also remembered that Tamara loved to sleep with Mom. So I asked Tamara if she wanted to sleep with me and Scandy. She jumped at the opportunity. I ran my hands through her hair and thought. What do I say to comfort her? What would Mom say? In that instant I remembered that when I was a child and slept with Mom, she would always ask if we had said our prayers.

"Did you say your prayers?" I asked Tamara.

"No, I didn't. Would you like me to say a prayer for all of us?"

She said a cute little child's prayer that went something like this: "God is good, God is great, please God take care of us. Amen."

"Great job, mama! If Mom was here she would be so proud of you. Mommy loved praying to God."

"Do you want to hear a quote from the bible?"

I was a bit thrown off because I had no idea she knew bible quotes. "Sure, momma, go ahead and shoot."

"For God so loved the world that he gave his only begotten son that he who believeth in him shall not perish but have everlasting life, John 3:16."

I was shocked. I couldn't quote the bible like that, and here's my baby sister quoting it verbatim. I congratulated her.

"Wow, mama, I'm so proud of you, and God and Mom are proud of you more. If Mom were here she'd love to hear you say that to her."

"I already told her that last week."

"What did she say?"

"She said that she wanted me to tell you that."

My hairs stood up, and I began to cry. I knew in that instant that Mom was with us. I felt overwhelmingly convinced that she was around us, guiding me to say the right things to Tamara and guiding Tamara to say the right things to me.

It was comforting. Mom was still here.

31

THE BUSINESS OF LIVING

Soon after Mom passed, it was time to move into our new apartment. Kira transitioned into her own apartment that she was able to obtain through some help from Diane. I felt like it was Mom who set it all up for us, like she was pulling strings from up above or we were carrying out some divine plan God had cooked up for us.

But then things got a bit bumpy. Once we settled in, I found out that Marisa was failing all of her classes, and Robert was following suit, from declining grades to failures across the board. At first I was able to deal with these issues. Then, after a while I felt a bit burdened. The amount of responsibility that was bestowed upon me became real—fast.

There were the real issues of schooling and children. Then was the issue of coping with loss, which both the kids and I were trying to do. It was overwhelming, but I thought, I can do this!

I counseled Marisa constantly. When that didn't work, I went to parent-teacher conferences to work with the school to try to re-engage Marisa in school. Whenever I attended follow-up conferences, I was told she was getting worse.

Here I was doing everything possible, and it wasn't helping.

To make things more stressful, Sara and Tamara were beginning to do poorly in the boarding school they were in. I would get at least one phone call a night with one or both of them crying and begging: "Please, Eddie, I hate it here. I just want to be with you guys. I miss Mommy."

I couldn't take it anymore and went to file a petition for custody. I felt that given the circumstances, we could be of greater support to one another if we were all living together. I felt bad that the girls had to deal with the death of their mother at a boarding placement they didn't like to begin with, so I'd be helping to relieve their stress.

Predictably, there was resistance from their grandmother and Aunt Cindy all over again. They felt like the only reason the kids wanted to leave was because they knew I was an option. They accused me of telling the kids to be bad on purpose for me to have a better case to get them.

How ridiculous! Here I was trying to deal with their emotional seesaws, trying to bring and keep the family together. Of course they chose not to believe me.

Against all odds, I won custody. Then the real battle began.

GOOD GUY, BAD GUY

All four felt like I wasn't their parent. They seemed to imagine it was going to be party time! No rules. After all, it was Eddie.

Being a parent was hard. I had to stand firm, and field their emotions and challenges. It was a constant battle. Turbulent, progressive madness.

I was a full-on parent now. My rules were simple. Go to

school and try to do well, clean your room, and you can do whatever the hell you want after that. But they wanted to sleep all day and hang out all night. Marisa continued to get worse in school to the point where her report card reflected that she only attended one of three months when I was sending her to school every day.

Robert began to fail more classes. Sara and Tamara were always making messes they didn't want to clean, and the food bills were ridiculously high. While they were in my custody, I was getting $550 a month in food stamps. Within a week or two all the food was eaten—I'd have to decide between eating for the next two weeks and paying the light bill. Every day that I came home the house was a mess, and I'd flip out and make everyone clean.

Then they'd all fight one another because none of them wanted to clean up. Instead of working as a team to clean up faster as I recommended, they would spend endless time blaming the messes on one another. When I took them clothes shopping, I had to shop at places like Conway's or anywhere cheap because that was all I could afford.

Here I was making a difference with the little I had and could do. But the reality was they did not see it that way. So they'd burst my bubble by saying things that hurt me.

"I can't believe we're bargain shopping!"

Sometimes it would just make me cry. Here I was trying to keep it all together. Getting them all in a nice family home! Scraping and budgeting. And all they could do was be lazy and whine.

Scandy and I would talk about it with them and try to humble them by explaining that we were doing the best we could with what we had. Scandy was a great support from the very beginning. He treated all the kids as though they were his brothers and sisters and never had a problem supporting them.

But there was no end to the phone calls from school. And then there were the calls from angry family members. The kids would go to each family member to try to get money by badmouthing me and acting like they had nothing at all. So I became Eddie the bad guy. Apparently, I used all of my money for personal expenses and neglected them in terms of clothing and food. It bothered me that the family had the wrong perception of what was going on.

I tried to ignore their whining. After all, what had they done to help? I knew I was doing the best I could with the limited resources available to me. I also knew that the apartment we lived in was actually pretty luxurious. Each room had a television and cable box, there was a 60-inch TV in the living room, and two computers, and regardless of how broke we were, there was always enough food. The apartment itself was such a blessing.

Then, besides the usual mess and headaches, the utility bills began to come in sky high. I'm talking $900 a month kind of high because we were responsible for heat and hot water as well as electricity. The kids didn't monitor their use when I wasn't home. Sometimes the house would be a sauna because the kids put the heat up to the max. When the apartment got hot, they would cool down by opening the windows. When I got mad and yelled at them for being inconsiderate, they'd just write the situation off as "Eddie being an asshole for no reason." I was beginning to get fed up with the situation.

EXHAUSTION

As time progressed the issues became more abundant. Sara and Marisa were getting into fights at school all the time. There were constant, even hourly phone calls from schools about how they were disruptive and not producing any work. And they would blame the teachers. Or claim that situations were against them. No matter what the evidence, they were innocent. Of course the little virgins never had homework.

And I was exhausted after work and after fielding all the calls and stresses of being a full-time parent. But they would be hanging out with a bunch of friends in the house without a heads-up. The house would be a wreck. In fairness to them, I said when they came home they were to do their homework, clean up after themselves, and then they could relax. That didn't work because the house was always messy. When I'd ask to review homework they'd lie and say that it was done and left at school. I put Marisa on a sign-in sheet, and she began signing her teacher's names fraudulently to act like she was compliant in school. That worked in her favor until I went to the next parent-teacher conference and found out that the sign-in sheets were fake.

It seemed that grieving, adjusting, and just being was a luxury. The business of living was full time. And the kids did not make it easy.

I was running out of options fast. Money was getting tighter and tighter. Scandy and I were working all the time only to come home to drama and bullshit from the kids. After a while the two smaller ones started doing whatever they wanted because they knew the bigger ones were getting away with it. Marisa pretty much dropped out of school, and Robert was hanging out at all hours of the night. This meant more drama and worry.

Tamara began to go to friends' apartments without permission, which I was strongly against because of fear of something happening to her. I continued to fight with them about these issues and nothing got better. In fact they were annoyed with me and my rules and felt I wasn't their father so they didn't have to listen to anything I had to say. I came home one day and found Tamara alone with a boy in the house, and I flipped out. I gathered them all together and had family talks about where things were and where they should be. When the talks didn't work, I'd threaten to have them removed by ACS, or worse, hit them if they continued to behave the way they were.

A MINI GANG WAR

I got a call at three o'clock on a Wednesday from Robert whose school was downtown in Manhattan. He was at Sara's school, which was further up in the Bronx. He said that they had been jumped by a bunch of kids there. I asked no questions and left work to rush to the Bronx. I went to the school ready to cut heads off of the school staff for being neglectful in protecting Sara. I called the police and made a report and everything. The staff apologized and said they would call me the next day to follow up. They assured me that the girls who jumped Sara, Marisa, and Robert would be suspended.

The next day at the school, after being called in to talk about next steps and delve deeper, the principal claimed that the police reversed the report on Sara and she now had a juvenile record for misconduct and falsifying a police report.

Also, Marisa and Robert weren't allowed around the school anymore because they were the ones who had started the fight. It was explained to me that on Monday, Sara was in class and threw a paper that hit a kid who then threatened to jump her after school. She called Robert, not me, and he in turn called Marisa.

So they staged their own mini gang war, and these were the consequences. Robert and Marisa jumped the girl who had threated Sara, and did it again the next day. On Wednesday they finally got jumped because the girl retaliated. That was it! I couldn't take the stress anymore.

HISTORY REPEATS

I had begun to get random icepick headaches and would scream from the pain. My stress levels were ridiculously high. I was getting nowhere fast. After all that we had been through, Marisa came home with a report card that showed every class not just failing but getting 50s and 45s. The teachers even told me that the numbers were only that high because the law prohibits them from putting the actual grades. When asking

Marisa what was wrong with her, she looked at me like she had an attitude. Her expression was as if this was routine, and she couldn't wait for me to shut up already.

With each incident that passed, I considered that, if I didn't make an example out of Marisa, the other ones were just going to get worse. I went to my room and grabbed a belt and hit her with it four times on her waist. I told her that from now on, I would hit her one time for every failing grade if she continued to cut school.

I was desperate. Nothing had worked. I thought that by doing so she would change her ways, and the others would realize that I meant business, so they would shape up. Well, I was wrong.

The next day while cooking dinner, I looked out my window to find three police cars parked outside. When my doorbell rang, I opened it to two ACS workers and about six police officers. I welcomed them into my home.

They explained that Marisa told the school that I was violent and she feared for her life. She also said that I beat her and showed them a mark on her waist from the belt I used. Of course she didn't say anything about why it was done. I asked that they give me a shot to explain things from my perspective. I showed them the bedrooms and the filth the girls refused to clean up. I showed them the entire apartment's amenities, cabinets full of food, and dinner waiting for the kids.

I explained what I did professionally (case management), and their perspective of the situation changed. The ACS workers went as far as to state that they had an entirely different picture of what the apartment and living situation was like based on the statements given to them. The officers told me that what I did was the right thing and that it was unfortunate that I had to be penalized for my actions because I was doing a hell of a job with the kids. But procedure for abuse allegations that are proven truthful included charging me in court. I was given court papers to go the next day, and the kids were removed.

I cried because I was regretful and I felt like I failed Mom. I couldn't keep it together even though I promised I would. The next day I went to court as requested, and while on my way I received a phone call from ACS. The worker said that they wanted to return the children to me and drop the abuse charges because Marisa had changed her position and the details of why the incident occurred. Apparently, after Marisa was told that she would be placed into a home, the truth came out and she asked to come back home with me.

32

THE SYSTEM
FAILS AGAIN
... AND AGAIN

I took the kids back, but things got worse. This time I had
no leverage. They knew that I could scream and shout but
couldn't hit them because I didn't want to go to jail. Things
continued to get worse, and the bills continued to pile up until
I contacted ACS myself and gave ACS an ultimatum: "You guys
help me financially and emotionally or I call it quits."

After doing so, an investigation was launched and a case
was opened. A worker was sent out to investigate our home,
and I was sure things would work out in my favor. What I
didn't anticipate was that the kids would pull the ACS worker
aside and lie about me so they could be removed. They did this
because they had planned to go to someone else's house to
live, where they could do whatever they wanted. They told the
ACS worker that I yelled at them all day and that I had money

for me but never for what they needed, and the list goes on. They really made me look bad, and then it happened almost overnight. I remember the ACS worker asking me: "Is there any way you will keep them in your home?"

"Yeah, when your agency provides me with the financial assistance I'm entitled to in order to support them."

She explained that I had custody of the children, and the only way to get benefits from fostering them is if they were foster children in the care of ACS—if I hadn't petitioned for custody, but instead for foster kinship status. I acted tough and stuck to my ground about receiving support from the system. She said that the children would be removed as soon as a placement was found. I let her leave and thought I would just withdraw from my decision if they didn't come through with the support.

MARIA

ACS decided to remove the kids, and when I asked to keep them, they took them anyway because of what the kids told them. They placed the kids in the old foster home they used to be in when we were originally taken from Mom back in 1998. This home was with a woman named Maria who was seventy-plus years old and in a wheelchair. By that point I was so frustrated and felt so betrayed that I decided to just move on with my life.

I had sweated blood to keep them all together. They didn't care!

Scandy and I moved out into a studio apartment on Marion Avenue. I continued to follow up on the kids regularly to monitor their progress. Interestingly enough, the poor old lady they went to live with called me all the time to ask me to come and discipline them because they were doing whatever they wanted. She would tell me of how they were throwing things at her, cursing her out, and wishing for her death.

Marisa officially dropped out of school and started doing

ecstasy. So did Robert, and predictably, he was failing all his classes. Sara dropped out of school and was smoking marijuana, and Tamara was failing all of her classes.

The situation with the kids never got better. In fact every time I called to check up on them, I knew I wouldn't get good news. Still I felt obligated to follow up because I wanted to keep at least some of the promise I'd made to Mom and because I actually care about them. These were my siblings whom I loved deeply. They were all I had.

When going to court to release custody to Maria, the judge indicated that in order for her to keep them, she would need to take a neglect charge because they weren't going to school. Maria began to cry and decided that it was best for the kids to get a higher level of care, so she withdrew from her petition. The judge then charged ACS to remove the children from her home immediately and place them separately because they were found to be of harm to one another. The ACS liaison asked that the courts give them until the following week to place the kids so they would have enough time to find appropriate placements. That week turned into a month, that month turned into a year, and as each month passed, things progressed to the point of no return.

A DIFFERENT APPROACH

My relationship with the kids had gone awry because they were sick and tired of hearing my mouth about school and what they needed to be doing for themselves. I myself was tired of sounding like a broken record. I decided to take a different approach and just be there for them as a support and not a parent. I would visit and hang out with the kids and hear the updates on how bad things were and try my hardest not to comment or show emotion. This was really hard. I had tried so hard to keep them together. But they seemed to be their own worst enemies. Acting out like kids do, but going beyond. Acting dysfunctional, fighting kids, skipping school and their responsibilities.

Scandy, Kira, and I pulled some strings and were able to get Robert and Marisa hired to work at Pret A Manger in Midtown. This was the British version of a Starbucks. They did well and were stable for the most part. Marisa finally obtained a GED and Robert started doing better in school.

MORE BAD NEWS

But Sara refused to re-enroll in school, and Tamara dropped out, too. Maybe a year and a half after ACS was told to place the kids, they still remained in the madhouse run by the poor, wheelchair-bound Maria. The kids' schools began to call ACS and make reports of educational neglect. Then the neighbors around Maria's house began to make reports that the kids were smoking marijuana and hanging out at all hours of the night. ACS launched an investigation and found the allegations to be true. Sara and Tamara were removed and placed in a mental health facility called Bayley Seton Hospital in Staten Island where they were to be evaluated.

I constantly called the ACS worker and argued that the kids weren't mentally ill but out of control because of the agency's failure to follow up. They argued that the kids had mental issues. This was to cover their own asses because they failed to follow up as the courts ordered.

Marisa was eventually fired from Pret A Manger for being late and calling out, and Robert dropped out of school to work full time. They were both still using ecstasy, and I could feel the pressure building to the point where I needed to act or I would probably lose one of my siblings. I visited Sara and Tamara often. It did not get better. Every time I got an update, the news was all bad. There was always something new and bad they were doing. I had been down this road. Oh God, if only I could show them the crystal ball I held.

I spoke with them as often as possible to warn them of the pending higher levels of care they would face if they continued to behave in the ways they were, but they didn't listen. As I spoke, more and more I could see them retreating, bent on a certain path of destruction.

RTC

One morning at work, I received a phone call from Marisa who told me that Sara had been placed into a residential treatment center (RTC) in Long Island after flipping out in Bayley Seton. Sara had been defending Tamara from a staff member who was being inappropriate to her, and they wound up fist fighting. When the police were called, Sara flipped out and was immediately removed by an   ambulance and taken to the RTC. No information was released to us as to where she was or when we could speak to her. I warned Tamara that she might face the same fate if she didn't begin to go to school and follow the rules there. When I followed up with the facility, I was informed that the staff member who fought with Sara had been removed and sent elsewhere to work.

As time passed, Tamara's behavior went from bad to worse. She got kicked out of school, after which her new treatment recommendation was an RTC as well. When asking the ACS workers if I could take her back, I was told that I couldn't because of the record of hitting Marisa.

But then, a few weeks after Sara was sent to the RTC, Sara called me, hysterically crying. We were both emotional at the contact. She was sorry for her behavior and really wanted to use the opportunity to grow and change, to live a normal life. I told her I was proud of her and couldn't wait to see her improve and return home.

33

CRISIS AND RECONNECTION

During this time, Robert started having health problems. One day he came over to Kira's house to hang out. He told us that he hadn't done ecstasy for almost a month and was stressed out because he was tired of supporting Marisa. Marisa didn't want to look for work and didn't want to stop doing ecstasy, and he was fed up. They had spoken about the issues he was having, and she didn't take it well at all. She cut him off and said that the family was dead to her because all we ever did was make her feel like shit.

We comforted him and explained that these were issues similar to the ones we faced while caring for them. We hung out for a while, and Scandy and I went home to sleep. The next morning we were woken up by a frantic phone call from Kira saying that Robert wasn't breathing, and they had just called an ambulance. Scandy and I were dressed and out the door in seconds. We drove as fast as we could. All I could think was, Oh my God, I'm going to lose my little brother now.

When we arrived, I saw the EMTs trying to wake Robert. He was conscious but not himself. They assured us that he had just had a seizure and he would be okay. We went to Jacobi Hospital, where he regained consciousness. The attending nurse ran blood tests and said that they all seemed normal. She went on to say that they needed to do an MRI, but since it was the weekend, they had to wait until the following Monday. I thought of this as an opportunity not only to reconnect with my little brother but to reconnect Marisa with all of us. I went to Maria's house and picked up her and Tamara (who was AWOL from the facility) and brought them to the emergency room where Robert was. I used the time to express the need for change with drug use and things of that nature.

After a few hours in the emergency room, Robert was released, and we all went to my apartment to hang out. We settled in, and Scandy and I decided to go get a haircut. Tamara and Marisa stayed home to watch Robert, and Kira and her girlfriend Jen went to go do their nails. While in the barber's chair, I received a frantic call from Tamara.

"Eddie, he's shaking! He's having another one! Eddie!"

She said that an ambulance was on the way. I flew out of the chair, jumped in my car, and raced back home to find another EMT trying to bring Robert back to consciousness. We all went to Montefiore Medical Center this time, where they said they wanted to keep him for monitoring.

That night I decided to stay with Robert at the hospital to watch over him and keep him company. Robert was adamant about leaving the hospital because he didn't want to be there. I refused to sign him out because I was concerned that he might have another seizure. As the time passed, we both fell asleep. About fifteen minutes later, I heard a loud thump, which jolted me into consciousness. I literally flew out of my bed to check on Robert. He had just fallen to the floor and was having a seizure. I screamed for a nurse at the top of my lungs.

She came in and started yelling for help. I grabbed Robert's head because as his body moved back and forth, his head was hitting the ground. Within twenty minutes, Robert was conscious again. He would stay overnight. I hugged my little brother. With each minute that passed, I reflected on the situation at hand. I couldn't help but think of where the rest of the kids' lives had gone and how much I was really needed in their lives.

Mom's passing had been followed by a whirlwind of tragic events. I began to realize it was not my role to be God and be able to control situations. Kids would be kids. Troubled kids, more so.

STABILIZATION

Robert stayed in the hospital for the next three days having all kinds of testing done to determine the cause of the three seizures. After doing an MRI, EEG, CAT scan, and blood work, the doctors had no answer! The results indicated that Robert was normal. He was discharged and placed on medications to prevent any further seizures.

Before leaving the hospital, I called Marisa to see where she was. When she answered her phone, she was crying. I asked what was wrong, and she told me that a guy who lived in her home had punched her in the face. I instructed her to call the police and told her I was on my way.

I jumped in the car and sped over to where the kids were staying. When I arrived, the police were taking a statement from Tamara and Marisa. When I was briefed on what happened, I was told that the guy also punched Tamara in the face. Both Marisa and Tamara had huge black eyes and bruises on their faces. I was furious! Tamara told me that he stole her Nintendo DS, and when Marisa asked if he took it, the guy flipped out and hit both of them. It was that situation in combination with Robert's that made me realize that I needed to take my siblings back.

I sent Tamara back to her facility because she was AWOL and made Marisa and Robert pack up all their stuff to bring to my house. I called ACS and left a voicemail indicating that I was taking them regardless, because the administration was continuously neglectful in following up on the children's welfare.

At home Scandy agreed that we needed to step in and take over. Immediately, we sat down and made plans to move into a new apartment to accommodate Robert and Marisa. For the next few days I did nothing but work and reflect on where I was in life.

Every time I thought about my mom, tears filled my eyes. I'm really trying, Mom. But it's so hard. Could I really handle them? I remembered the horrible headaches, the calls from the schools, the kids acting out. So I made a list. What went wrong? How could I prevent this? What I did, what they did. After reading the list over and over, I realized that this was it. I could do it, but I just needed to pace myself and approach the children as their role model brother and not their father.

The children's ACS worker called me back eventually and informed me that I couldn't take Robert because of the record of hitting Marisa. She indicated that Kira could take Robert, and I could take Marisa because she was of age (eighteen) to decide whom she wanted to live with. She also stated that ACS needed to consult with their attorney before making any final decisions. I argued that I didn't care what they had to say. The only reason they needed to speak to their lawyer was because they'd dropped the ball and wanted to cover their own asses. I also warned that I would seek legal counsel and sue them for neglect for letting the kids go for so long without any kind of follow-up.

Having Marisa in my home, Robert in Kira's, and Sara and Tamara in an RTC really helped lighten the stress load for me. I liked that I could tackle Marisa first because she was the oldest and had the potential to take care of herself. I made a plan with Marisa to address her immediate needs as I would with any of my clients at work. This was going to be my new approach to things at home: case management without almost any emotions. Within a week of Marisa living in my home, she accomplished the little things I had been pushing for her to do for years prior. She was able to obtain a NYS identification card, open up a welfare case to begin receiving assistance until she obtained employment, and begin looking for a job with the new resume we helped her put together. Progress!

Then I was able to focus more on the long-term goal of getting Sara and Tamara back. And again it was December. The third anniversary of Mom`s death approached.

34

THE SUN
WILL RISE

At first it was rocky. I was dealing with everything that had just transpired with the children, work, the third anniversary of Mom's passing, and trying to find an apartment to move into. I realized that I needed to sign up for school for the spring semester. (I had been promoted at work on the condition that I work toward getting a college degree in business management.) I did so and signed up for a few classes to accelerate my education. This was also a part of my trying to lead by example, because I wanted the kids to pursue a higher education.

Thinking of Mom really helped me to put things into perspective. All I could think of was Mom's voice telling me that God would make sure I was okay.

"Have faith, Eddie spaghetti. It'll all work out."

I realized that I was a completely different person now. I saw that things could've turned out a lot worse. I could've become a drug dealer, been incarcerated, lost my mind, and the list goes on. The fact that I had been successful in obtaining and maintaining my case manager job was a blessing in itself.

In the process of mourning, I had the comfort of knowing I still had six pieces of Mom! My beloved, complex siblings . . . and it seemed that Mom used them to communicate with me and let me know that she was still around.

Even today, whenever I'm in a financial bind or something devastating happens, I know it is the storm before the calm. I know in my heart that my mom is here, watching over me to give me that extra little push I need to get through. I now realize that I am beyond blessed just to be alive. I am even more blessed to have met a man who supports me unconditionally and loves everything about me.

I used to want to be rich, have a huge house, and possibly be famous, but now I just ask my creator to let me live to see one more day. When I view my siblings doing things that they shouldn't be doing, I remind myself that they are just being young, growing up and learning every day. I can't do anything to change that except be there for them. I can only be a support and change the things I have control over. Looking back at my life has made me humble and grateful. After all, I have such a large family and strong support system. With every moment I move forward, I try to convince myself to think positive. My cup remains half full. It must. I refuse to think of the bad, the what ifs . . .

Even though the day to day was still rocky, I knew the future had great things in store for Scandy, my siblings, and me. I just needed to stay focused and remain optimistic. I realized that I could use my experience to grow and to try not to make any mistakes twice. Helping people isn't something that I just do for a living. It is something that is embedded in my DNA! It is my purpose, just as suffering abuse and being in a really bad system was part of the path that brought me here.

I love to feel like my purpose is being carried out with every breath I take. That's not say it isn't constant work to stay positive. Even years after my mom's death, I still wake up sometimes to an overwhelming sense of anxiety. The reality that everything I have built up for myself and my family could be taken away at any moment haunts me. The fear of losing my job or sanity still lingers in my thoughts. Although I combat that anxiety with the faith and determination to succeed, that voice of anxiety that is always in my head . . . Eddie, what's next? What do you need to prepare for?

35

FOSTER CARE

Life has a funny way of keeping me on my toes. As far back as I can remember I've had to worry about where my next meal was coming from, where I was going to stay, and who was going to hurt me. For the moment, though, I was stable, housed, and had loved ones around me that I, for the most part, trusted. With Marisa safe and making progress, I used this newfound stability to continue to fight for the rest of my siblings.

My lawyer decided it would be best for me to become a foster parent so that if things went seriously wrong, I could just place the kids back in the system with no neglect or abuse charges to justify the removal. It would also provide financial means to care for them, considering Scandy and I couldn't really afford to support them on our own.

The proceedings commenced but soon hit a road block. That old child abuse allegation from Marisa stayed on record and was found to be true since I'd admitted to hitting her. I filed for the record to be expunged and ultimately, after six months, had it removed from my record as well as from Scandy's. (It turns out that if you are an adult in the household of someone who was found guilty of child abuse, then you also get a record. He was pretty upset about it. His dream job was to become a school teacher. The possibility of not being able to become one shook him up a little.)

Scandy and I attended foster care courses that were required for me to become certified. After ten weeks and an intense investigation from ACS, we were cleared to have Sara come back to live with us. She had done well and learned from the RTC experience, and was ready to get back into school and stop smoking marijuana. Kira and Scandy pulled some strings at Pret again to get Marisa re-hired. Robert got fired after a "no call, no showing." (Sadly, he and I haven't really had much of a relationship after I placed the kids' fate back in the hands of the system while getting foster care certified.)

Foster parenting has its benefits and drawbacks. Funds were provided monthly via a check in the mail to cover any expenses related to caring for Sara. However, it came with a worker who monitored the household with monthly visits to ensure everything was okay. This annoyed me because I felt like I was being constantly supervised and judged and was tired of ACS being involved in my life.

After all, the system had failed me and removed me from my beloved mom. I felt like they were directly and indirectly the reason we were all in this mess to begin with. They removed us from Mom, she lost herself, and in turn we all lost her both physically and mentally. The reality was in order to keep the bills paid and food on the table, I needed to comply with the administration's demands.

So the frustration was with not being able to begin the healing process, as one would constantly be reminded that the ride wasn't over.

SET UP TO FAIL

I fought for Tamara, but she wasn't progressing the way Sara did at her RTC placement. Tamara was placed at Graham Windham School in Yonkers where the kids pretty much did what they wanted and the staff didn't really give a shit. I made sure to visit her every chance I had. I admit it was hard, making trips up at least once a week to meet with her social worker and therapist, having family therapy sessions with her, and trying to be a support for her to promote a change in her behaviors. I always felt bad for Tamara, because I realize that she had it worse than all of us put together. She was removed from Mom at birth for Christ's sake. She was born addicted to heroin and raised by a grandmother she knew as her mother until she was able to understand the difference. And when she finally got wind of who Mom was, Mom died. I tried to be empathetic, but some of the stuff she was doing was way out of control.

I was informed by the social worker that she was a member of the Blood gang, and was smoking marijuana and selling drugs on campus. She bunked school and traveled wherever she pleased, whenever she wanted. She was always out of the facility, running the streets and returning after a few days, and no one ever knew where she was going. One time the facility was contacted by the police because she and some other girls ran a bill up in Applebee's and ran out of the restaurant without paying.

Still, I felt I could make a difference by being there for her. I fought tooth and nail and even convinced the therapeutic staff that their diagnosis was off. I argued that her behaviors were because she was never stabilized in a home long enough to see real progress. It was my assessment that all of her behavior was a cry for attention and a result of her pain.

The sad thing, though, was that I was fighting both the facility and Tamara. I was constantly reminded by the social workers that she persisted in saying she did not want to live with me because she could not deal with my rules. I never stopped to pause and realize that this was because of her own inner demons, her need to act out and rebel. It had zilch to do with Eddie´s rules. The recommendation of the staff was to increase her level of care to a lock-down RTF facility where she would be placed with the worst kids there are.

I fought that, too, however, and her level of care was reduced to justify her being placed in my home under my supervision. I explained to Tamara that she needed to go to school and adhere to my rules and she would be fine. The understanding when I fought for her was that she would be placed in my home with schooling and funds for her in place. However, she came to the house with no school spot and no funds. I took Tamara shopping and maxed out my credit cards to show her that I would reward her for good behavior, but she wouldn't get anything if she gave nothing.

"If you work for something, you earn a reward. And if you work at nothing, then you earn nothing," I explained. " Simple, right?"

Initially, she adhered to my rules. I tried to set up her schooling but decided that regular school wasn't the way to go. After several attempts to find local vacancies failed, I felt this was a sign. So I took her to the Department of Education and was immediately turned around because ACS didn't give me any paperwork to show that I was authorized to care for her. After weeks of complaining and phone calls, I was assigned to an educational coordinator to assist me in the process. She and I worked together closely for a month, attending appointment after appointment. And all the while Tamara was home, bored all day. This compounded matters, so I challenged her. I gave her words to look up and define and use in sentences as work to keep her busy. Sometimes she did the assignments, and sometimes she didn't. When she didn't, I would ask why, and she would give me one of those looks that took me back to when I had the kids originally. A blank stare meaning, "Back off, Eddie. I'm pissed."

I maintained my stance, tried to stay calm, and made her complete any tasks she had—if she didn't, she had a detention type of punishment, such as having to write I didn't do it because . . . many times. I repeatedly complained to the agency's director that they had set me up for failure after my months of planning to make sure they didn't do exactly that.

The education specialist and I planned it so that Tamara would be given special schooling funded by the DOE where she would attend classes staffed by licensed therapists and social workers. She would be given incentives and therapy tailored around her individual history and would be in classes with only seven other kids, max ten. The only catch was that the process for acceptance after the interview was a month long. That would make it two whole months Tamara was not in school. We had no other options.

After that month we went back only to be told that they couldn't accept her yet because I signed an authorization that should have been signed by the agency's director.

Bullshit bureaucracy! Let's drag this out because we can! I contacted the agency, and they said it was protocol to obtain a signature from Steve, who was still incarcerated, so I had to wait until they got it. They had tried, but Steve said he wanted an attorney. He said it was because he was scheduled to be released in a few weeks, and he didn't want to sign anything.

This really pissed me off. He was an absent parent and yet couldn't even take a moment to sign a document. He messed up my life and Mom's. How the fuck could he have a say?

Why? Why does this man continue to make my life harder and all I'm trying to do is get Tamara into a special school? I argued that Tamara was good but growing impatient and bored with every day that passed. They insisted there was nothing they could do. I wasn't being compensated yet for Tamara's care, and my funds were growing tighter with each passing day. But I persevered.

She constantly asked for company (kids from the RTC who

we felt were bad influences) or to sleep over at people's homes (which we didn't have the authorization to the give permission for). Every time she asked, we patiently explained why we had to say no.

But being separated from her friends made her more frustrated and isolated. One day when I arrived home from work, Tamara wasn't home.

"Tamara? Are you hiding?"

I panicked and called everyone, but no one knew where she was. I called the agency and was instructed to call the police. I did so and filed a missing persons report. A couple of days later, Tamara showed up at the agency and said she refused to come back to my house because she couldn't deal with my rules. The agency explained that she had no choice, and she was escorted home.

As she entered the apartment, the energy in the room was eerily calm. A pregnant silence followed. Phrases curled and receded in the air, in my mind. No good could come of this discussion.

She barely looked at me.

"Where were you?"

"Don't worry about it!"

I got pissed and explained that as her caretaker, I needed to know where she was at all times to be able to protect her. It was no good. All lecturing and interrogating, for lack of a better word, i got no results. A conference was scheduled to discuss the runaway episode, and it was mandatory. I hate "mandatory" when it comes from ACS because these meetings are always scheduled without discussion as to what I had scheduled (like work), and they would put more stress on me because I didn't want them to have any reason to try another separation. The meetings also created a platform that I felt allowed Tamara to act out. If the system wasn't involved to begin with, she wouldn't feel so free to come and go as she pleased. She was so used to being moved around and in and out of facilities, that she didn't really have any concept of real-world consequences or what it was like when adults truly cared about her well-being. I feared that without consequences, she would just continue to keep running away.

The reality that this might not work, again, was almost too much for me to handle. Dear God and beloved Mom, Why is it that this is always so difficult and full of drama? Am I supposed to fail?

I tried to interact with Tamara, but I was the bad guy, the one who had the rules. So the energy between us was not good. She could not stand living with me, wanted out, and was waiting for the meeting so she could be done with this living arrangement. That was all. The conference date came, and Tamara and I met with a few social workers to discuss everything. The question was posed: "Where do we move from here?"

"I would like Tamara to answer that," I said. "For the past few years, I have been making the case for placement with me, but this time I want Tamara to make her case for what she wants. And I love and support her regardless of what she has to say."

Tamara resisted, but after prying, she said, "I want to go live with my dad or be placed somewhere else. I don't want to live with them."

I was crushed. It hurt to hear those words. I felt stupid. Why am I fighting for kids that don't respect me, don't respect themselves, and want to just do what they want? I began to cry.

"Why, Tamara? Because I want you to be home safe with us instead of on the streets? Because I want you to go to school?" I pointed to everyone in the room. "You see these people? They are paid to care about what happens to you, but at the end of their work shift, they go back to their families and completely forget about you. They don't truly care! I do! Why can't you see that I love you and only want the best for you? This is sad because they're going to place you now, and if you continue doing what you're doing with this rebel lifestyle, YOU are just going to keep hopping from facility to facility until they increase your level of care to a mental ward and YOU ARE NOT CRAZY or STUPID!"

The worker then asked me, "What do you want to do?"

I really wanted to say she was to stay with me, but I realized that my health, sanity, and even criminal (child neglect/abuse) record were all at stake. If I continued trying to pull her in my direction, she would just push away more, and it wasn't going to work for either of us.

"If she wants to leave, then I don't want her to, but I can't fight someone when the goal is to help them. So if she wants out, then give her what she wants."

I was emotional at first, but her face was stone cold, like she just did not care and was tired of hearing my mouth. With every word I spoke, I felt her become more and more defensive. My words had no impact. The workers said I needed to give them ten days, and they would have a new placement.

Over those days, I would say random things to her like, "You know living here would've been so sweet. You sure you want to go?"

She would just smile but change the subject. Again, the understanding was she wanted out. I could tell something inside of her wanted to stay, but the freedom she would gain from leaving weighed heavily on her decision.

And so I lost my sweet Tamara to the system. To her own demons.

36

WALDO

During this turbulent time of getting Sara and losing Tamara, I was offered the opportunity to participate in an all-expense-paid, ten-month certification for a CASAC-T (Credentialed Alcohol Substance Abuse Counselor in Training), a 350-hour course. After completing that certification, one can test to become a full CASAC recognized internationally and by the state. I jumped on the opportunity because my supervisor was awesome and allowed me to take the courses on Thursdays and Fridays while at work. What I found interesting was that my first module of training happened to be on family systems theory. Amazingly, it coincided with taking the girls back. It gave insight on how families work, giving me more skills and tools to work with. The coursework dived into roles, rules, boundaries, and overall family dynamics. It gave me a whole new perspective on my own family and how much trauma we had all experienced. I learned that it affected how we interacted with each other. I learned that trauma is recorded by the brain and if left unaddressed, can cause a variety of issues like drug use/abuse, promiscuity, and mental health issues like PTSD.

This left me with a few burning questions that I have asked myself regularly . . . What is my end result (other than pot use)? What is my trauma causing me to be like in my adulthood? I know I have trust issues, but what else is wrong with me? Am I going to lose my mind one day? Will I ever see a future? Will this virus kill me before I make it to become something of worth? Will I ever be successful or fall to my circumstances like everyone around me? So besides acquiring new and valuable skills, I could self-analyze, creating my own therapy.

One of the most valuable lessons I think I received from the training was what they called being aware of "Waldo." They taught us that like Waldo, we were all Waldos and Waldettes in this world trying to find ourselves. We should always remain aware of where we are, how we interact with people, and what is really going on within, especially when someone or something affects us emotionally. Doing so would ensure that the Waldo within remained in a growth state and really took advantage of this experience we call life.

GENOGRAMS

The training also helped me to explore my family history through a genogram. A genogram is something like a family ancestry chart, where you first list your parents and their parents and all the relatives you can think of. Then you identify any divorces, separations, deaths, addictions, legal troubles, mental health issues, physical health issues, and lack of supports specific to each relationship and individual. The results can be quite impactful—the genogram outlines glaring patterns throughout your family history that are pervasive regardless of whether you have active relationships or interactions with past generations. In other words: blood carries more patterns than you may think.

When completing the genogram, I found that there were several commonalities within my family history that included substance abuse, domestic violence, large households with many children, and a lack of either one parent figure or both. This immediately put my life into perspective. My siblings and I were victims of our family history. There were so many health and mental health issues; patterns of absentee fathers and parents dying young; instances of tobacco, alcohol, and substance abuse; cycles of physical abuse, sexual abuse, and neglect; cheating husbands and wives, and the list goes on. That made me wonder, Are we doomed because it's embedded in our DNA to repeat these behaviors and live such lives?

It became my goal to save at least one of my siblings—or accept that some things in life are greater than me. After all, I could not control everything, but I could at least be accountable for my actions. I couldn't help but feel like this was Mom's and God's way of giving me insight to further equip me to take care of my family. Or at least to become aware of what was really going on outside my emotions and perceptions. Outside of my past as a child. Outside of the horrible childhood experiences.

I realized I was trying to compensate and make things right, but so much damage had been done that it was out of my control. Juggling work, class, and family became more difficult as time progressed toward my graduation. Over the course of the ten months, I obtained Tamara and went through that whole experience. The graduation, coinciding with Tamara's removal, felt almost like a sign. With Tamara about to be removed yet again I could feel that load of typical day-to-day stress building to a pitch! This was angst!

Again my self-esteem was challenged. Eddie was failing again. Eddie the caregiver could not save his baby sister.

But a piece of me had grown enough to step back. I

understood that this was not my fault but a result of many factors, including the behavior exhibited by my siblings. They made choices, and they needed to face the consequences of those choices. If not, then I would essentially be a part of the problem, because I'd be enabling their behaviors. All I could do was be supportive and remind them that regardless, I was here for them.

GRADUATION DAY

As graduation day approached, I began to invite family members to the ceremony. It was a credential (not a degree), but more than I'd ever expected to accomplish, and I wanted my siblings to be front row in the audience. I wanted to share the experience of accomplishment with them. On graduation day, I called everyone (Dad and his girlfriend, Kira, Marisa, and Scandy). I had no way of reaching Robert but hoped he'd hear about it through the girls and would show up.

When I spoke to Kira, she said she was on her way and would see me there. When I spoke to Marisa, she said she didn't feel like going, and it pissed me off, but I wrote it off as a lie because I thought she was going to surprise me. I was so excited—every grueling eight-hour class had led up to this great day ten months later. I'd observed groups of graduates during their ceremonies every month prior and pictured what mine would be like.

A few minutes before the ceremony began, Sara and Scandy arrived alone. Immediately, I got mad but thought everyone else was hiding somewhere and would surprise me last minute. As the ceremony started, I had to accept a no-show. I felt let down. During the ceremony I kept thinking of how selfish and cruel it was for Kira and Marisa not to show up. Here I was all these years, busting my ass to provide and be supportive in anything they did, and the one time I needed them to support me, they weren't there.

I realized that I was fighting for everyone all by myself.

Why fight for people who not only hurt themselves constantly, but let me down time and time again? Especially the one time it really meant something to me.

When it was my turn to accept my credential and receive feedback from my peers, I said, "First of all, I'd like to thank God and my mother for this. I have learned so much more about counseling and addiction than I already knew, but what I value more than anything else I've learned is having been made aware of Waldo. I've learned who the real Waldo is and that I always have to check in on him because he grows, changes, and digresses every day. This experience has given me more than a credential; it has strengthened my knowledge of self so that I can become the model of a man my mother always told me I would be. The man I strive to be so that I can be an amazing counselor, friend, family member, and human being. It feels weird to have come from nothing, feeling like a nobody, and thinking I would never be anything to now feeling like I have more than I have ever dreamed of in all effects of my life. The Universe, God, or however you all identify with your higher power has a funny way of putting people, places, and random things in one's life path. As a result I have been blessed with a supportive, amazing man and a crazy, dysfunctional, but unique family who keep me on my toes literally all of the time. I have also been blessed with amazing friends, colleagues, and associates. Thank you all for helping to shape Waldo into the man he is and will someday be."

I cried. It was inevitable. So did about fifty others. That, too, was inevitable. People cared, were moved . . . The fact that they were not my siblings was a side issue.

Wow, they actually hear me and my struggle. I sobbed silently, for Mom, for my life that was, for the now. For my new self!

The floor opened up for feedback, and to my surprise one after another they began to praise me for being an inspiration to them and for being a pleasure to be around. I even got feedback from people I thought didn't like me and they actually did. I was told how funny I was, that I was strong, and the sky was the limit for me. I couldn't help but be humbled by the overwhelming amount of positivity they gave me. Then Sara raised her hand and stood up to speak.

"Hi, I'm Sara, and I'm Eddie's sister. I just wanted to say that he's an awesome brother and has been there for me when no one else was." As she continued, she burst into tears. "I love him, and he took me into his home, put me into school, and takes care of me. I love you, Eddie."

Wow, what a feeling, I thought. I felt validated after so many years of feeling unappreciated. Yet the truth is I needed no one's validation, except God's. But I was so surprised by her raw emotion and proud of her for being there for me. It was in that moment that I realized that if no one else showed up, that was okay, because Scandy and Sara had. And if Sara was the only person I was reaching, then that was okay, too. At least I could save one.

When I got home that day, Marisa told me that the ACS worker had shown up early to remove Tamara and place her elsewhere. I immediately felt saddened but was comforted by the news that she was being placed with a female foster parent. I thought maybe there was no connection—I might be gay, but I'm not a woman. Maybe she needed a female parental figure to guide her.

And with Tamara's departure, the chaos lessened at home. The only issues we faced now were the typical ones, with the house being dirty (because no one ever cleaned but me) and Marisa not paying her portion (fifty dollars a week) on time, ever. It was nothing new for Marisa to fail to meet her promises, but it aggravated me every week to have to have talks with her about her lack of responsibility. On the upside, Sara began to step up to the plate by cleaning the house, which lightened my load of stress.

PERVASIVE PATTERNS

After five and a half years being with her girlfriend Jennifer, Kira finally decided to let her go. Jen had been an alcoholic, and Kira had had enough. She had lost her job and as a result of that, lost her apartment. So she decided to move in with us to get back on her feet.

I knew this would be an interesting and challenging transition for all of us. I couldn't help but be reminded of the family systems theory I'd learned during my training. Whenever a member moves into the household or out of it, it threw off the balance in roles, which would be redefined with each composition change, to ultimately create a new equilibrium. Within months Kira went from being depressed and hopeless to progressing and gaining new employment, where she ultimately thrived, becoming an assistant manager who ran a business. She is currently advancing and excelling in her career. I am proud of her and will always be.

Having everyone living together sounded ideal, but in fact it was all chaos! The different emotional wavelengths, agendas, and diverse ages and levels of maturity—come on! I always try to keep this in mind when approaching my family but cannot help feeling frustrated when it seems like I'm the only one who cares. I often thought about my future and whether or not I would have one if I continued to spend all my time worrying about everyone else.

As I continue to grow up, the reality that my past is over seems like a dream and a curse. Eddie, all grown up. No one can ever physically abuse me again. But Mom has been gone for almost six years. So exactly who is Eddie? What is his purpose? Why did Mom have to die?

I guess I still view Mom's passing as a curse, a punishment.

It's funny how God has a way of removing one blessing but replacing it with another. Now before I go on, I must issue this disclaimer: No one will EVER replace the warmth, love, and genuine care that my mother gave me. She is missed and thought of daily.

But over the years Scandy and I figured out how to bring

our families together. Scandy lost his father at the age of ten, and I had lost my mother—but we still had my father and his mother for parental figures. And Scandy's mother is awesome, and I love her very much. From the start, she always showed me love and treated me like I'm her own son. Hell, she and I speak more than she speaks to Scandy.

And so, as Scandy's family became my family, and my family found its new normal, the forever emptiness started to fade.

PART
FOUR

CLOSURE

37

DAD

When dad came back into my life for real, around the time I was working on my credential, it was confusing at first. He was a different man. Perhaps he dove into his own Waldo. Whatever it was that prompted it, I'm glad he changed his ways.

I realize now that like me, he experienced his own trauma and dealt with people accordingly. When he was locked up and we never visited him, that left him feeling vulnerable. "How come when anybody needed me I was there, but when I needed somebody, no one was there for me?" It felt like an echo. I have explained to him that I was a child and was busy trying to survive in the world. I think he understands that, but he still has difficulty accepting the reality that his children were left with a man who abused them and he was helpless in the situation. Anyway, that is my assessment.

Out of the blue I received phone calls and text messages asking me to come over and hang out. "Come over and have dinner, just come over!"

It was uncomfortable at first considering my own insecurities—I never really knew how he felt about me being gay. He always said he didn't care about it, but interacting with him had been awkward. I am a very emotional person, quite the opposite of Dad. However, I give credit where credit is due. I really love my father and am willing to put the past behind us to move forward with optimism about our relationship. Hanging out with Dad is an experience now. I continue to learn things about him I never knew. He tells me stories of his past as a teenager before he went to prison, and my eyes light up like a little kid in a candy store.

He's actually a cool, down-to-earth guy. He doesn't care that I smoke pot, so long as I take care of myself and maintain my responsibilities as a man.

My favorite thing about my dad is his cooking! Man, can this guy cook. Initially I was reluctant to eat his food because he was known for being a health nut. He doesn't eat red meats, fatty foods, fried foods, fast foods, partially hydrogenated oils, or anything that isn't whole wheat, and the list goes on. He drinks only water and goes to gym religiously. He values his health and his freedom and lives a simple life now, enjoying each day that passes.

Knowing all of this, I thought his food would suck. But I was in a phase where I was eating smarter and working out, so I tried it. To my surprise it was the best homemade food I had eaten in years! Everything tasted so fattening and delicious but was 100 percent good for you. With each visit to his house, I craved Dad's food more and more.

Then, just when I thought I had learned it all, he whipped out dessert! He makes all kinds of stuff covered in honey glazing and dark chocolate. Yum! Then he adds cranberries and nuts, and oh my gosh, this is heavenly stuff. It felt so bad yet tasted so good.

Dad's (now ex-) girlfriend of seven years, Vanessa, is pretty awesome too. She's a nurse and is beautiful. She's very loving and caring and has a heart like that of Jesus. She kind of reminded me of Mom sometimes when she would speak of God. (Dad, on the other hand, always references the devil and says he is his son. I pray for Dad. Is he joking?) I love Vanessa because she loves me and accepts me into her life. Also, I know she has had significant influence on my dad and has loved him and supported him since his release from prison.

Hanging with Dad is always fun, especially when reminiscing of old times. His friends/co-defendants are being released one after the other, and they have this brotherly bond that is inspiring. Dad pays his blessings forward and offers his friends jobs working with him in construction. He buys them clothing to help them get back on their feet. Every time they're around, I feel like a little kid. It takes me back to when they were cooking and bagging up crack while I played my video games. I know it sounds weird, but that's what I think of.

What truly amazes me from time to time is when I observe Dad . . . and I see him act and behave like I do. This is fascinating to me, considering I grew up without him. Yet the way he thinks about responsibility, life, and overall caution in certain situations is exactly the way I think and act in those situations. For example, I played with Scandy all the time and would tease him with pet names (you know, lover stuff), and when dad played with Vanessa, he does the same thing.

So we are genetically linked and have similar traits. That genogram from school pops up in my head. I wonder, Is my personality derived from his DNA? Am I going to be bitter and angry at the world when I am his age?

Dad continues to surprise us. For example, Thanksgiving is something we (Scandy, my siblings, and I) always celebrate at my house. We spent it once with Dad at Vanessa's mom's house when we first started to interact, but it held no true emotional significance to me, even though it was the first time we'd spent it with him.

But Thanksgiving 2011 was different. Since the invisible wall of communication had been broken down, Dad asked us early on to spend it with him. We agreed and looked forward to the food and experience. When the day arrived and we got to his house, we were shocked at how much time, effort, and love was put into the dinner and overall experience. He had everything from rented tables and chairs to loads and loads of food and desserts. Kira, Scandy, and I kept harassing him to hurry with the food setup so we could get to eating. My grandmother (Dad's mom) was there, and so were all my siblings including Tamara. It was perfect. I felt like life was beginning to be normal. When we sat and ate, man was it great! Dad likes to stand around and watch us eat. It gives him thrills to see everyone enjoying his food, and it gives us thrills to eat it. I spent the rest of the night thinking about the reality that Dad was back and here to stay. My mind wandered to Mom, wishing she had lived. I was glad that Kira was finally afforded a father figure, and I could move back into the position of just being her brother.

Christmas rolled around. Usually Scandy and I bought everyone close to us, the whole lot. Pretty much every year from when we could afford to, we bought gifts. But we never got anything from anyone except Scandy's mother. Not that we expected anything—though I guess it would have been nice.

In 2011 we decided, based on our budget, that we couldn't buy gifts for everyone. Therefore we wouldn't buy anyone anything. Then I got an invite from Dad to spend Christmas with him. We agreed and planned to go to Scandy's mother's home in Pennsylvania for Christmas Eve/Christmas morning and then to Dad's on Christmas Day. After some discussion and re-budgeting, we changed our minds and put money together to buy everyone gifts. I could feel this inner child in me bursting with excitement to finally spend the holidays with my dad. I also felt bad for Scandy, knowing he missed his dad—but at least he had mine. That's another thing I have to give my Dad credit for, he really loves Scandy and treats him like he's his son. (Although they have this joking thing where Scandy says, "Hi, Dad," and Dad almost always replies, "I'm not your fucking father." It sounds bad, but when you see and hear it, it's all in fun and love. I think that through Dad's growth, he has realized that some of the ways he plays can be taken out of context, so as of recently he hasn't been replying in the same vein.)

When Christmas morning arrived, we drove back down to New York to go to Dad's. Upon arrival, to our surprise, Dad had his living room loaded, but like seriously loaded, with a ridiculous number of gifts. Holy shit, this is a lot of gifts.

He cautioned that they weren't all for us because he'd invited my aunt Ella, my grandmother, Vanessa's family, and all of us to be together to open our gifts. When he told me how many people were coming, I realized we shared something else in common: the joy of having everyone, family and friends, gathered in good fun. I'm a family man and behold, so is my father! He took the time and energy to put together not one but two major holidays back to back just to bring his family together and show love.

He made us wait all day while he prepared a feast, as usual. We didn't get to open our gifts until around 7 p.m., but I have to say, this was by far the best Christmas I'd ever had! He took gift by gift and distributed them by name. One by one, he made our night. He bought everybody really nice gifts. I got a Coach iPad case, some nice shirts, and an Apple TV. I was ecstatic! I had wanted this TV for a year. He took the time to investigate what I wanted. And I love my technology. Dad knew that.

Dad gave Scandy a pair of Coach gloves and a few hats and shirts. Kira got a Coach bag, Marisa got a Coach bag, and my aunt and cousins all got hooked up too. I felt bad for Aunt Ella, who cried in joy. I could tell she had been going through a lot, and this was a breath of fresh air for her. That's the funny thing about karma. She supported Dad when he was in jail. Whenever she could, she would send food packages or money, and now that he was out, he essentially returned the favor. The energy in the room was phenomenal. I was so tired from screaming and laughing so much. Thanks, Dad.

I told my dad I loved him and gave him a hug. And he replied, "I love you, too, son." That moment felt surreal. Did my dad just say he loved me? Was he sick or dying?

I sent him a text the next day. "Thank you, dad. It's great to have you back in my life. It means a lot more than you know and has a positive effect on my life. I'm glad you're back."

He replied, "Ditto". I remember looking at my phone and smiling and tearing up. This was what I always wanted and prayed for as a child. I wanted my dad to love me and be in my life, and now he finally was.

As New Year's approached, Dad invited us to spend it with him and Vanessa at her mom's house. She always brought in the New Year with her mom. We explained that we'd already agreed to spend it with Scandy's mom and his family but decided to test the waters and invite him over as well. Dad said he would come, but there was a piece of me that kind of didn't believe it.

But when the day arrived, he asked us to stop by Vanessa's mom's to eat and then he would come with us to Scandy's family's place. We did so, and to my surprise, he got in my car and came with us to meet Scandy's family. He'd met some of them briefly in the past but never in this type of setting. When we approached the door, I was overwhelmed with anxiety. I didn't want anything to go wrong. I just wanted everyone to get along and mesh well.

God is good because they all loved Dad and Vanessa. Scandy's mom was excited to have them there, and so was the rest of the family. I could see that Dad and Vanessa were not only comfortable but overwhelmed by the level of warmth and the reception they'd received. It all worked out. Scandy's cousin Irma even gave them gifts when they were about to depart. The holiday season couldn't have been any better—unless, of course, Mom had been there. But it was enough for me!

The feeling of having my Dad around is somehow comforting. It fills a void I didn't know was there until it was filled. I'm sure there will be many challenges to come, but they will be that much more acceptable with him in my life.

I love you, Dad, and thanks for being there for me. I'm sure we will have our challenges in getting to know each other, but I look forward to building on what we already have. I know it is difficult being a father figure when you don't know how to. All that matters is that you try.

38

POPS
AND SELMA

Life has a funny way of throwing you curveballs, and karma can fuck you or make your day. Take my grandparents and Steve, for example. I spent all my life wishing for the day when I could grow up and send them all to hell— and then I grew up and cut them all out of my life completely. Only to come to the conclusion that I don't hate them, and I forgive them. In fact, I feel horrible for ever hating them in the first place. Let me explain.

When growing up, I hated that Pops monitored his refrigerator. If we opened it, he ran out of his room to see who opened it and what they were taking out. I made a promise to never be greedy with food, to always share food with anyone who was hungry. Then I grew up and took the kids in on a low income, and reality set in. If people eat whatever, whenever, then there would be nothing to eat: lesson learned. Don't get me wrong. I still share my food with anyone who comes through my door without hesitation. I just understand now that Pops was not only caring for us while we stayed in his home, but he was providing food for Steve, Mom, and all of us on a small budget.

Selma also cared for us whenever Pops couldn't do so anymore, and this created feelings of resentment toward us. Of course, I still feel that the level of blame and hate leveled at my mother was unnecessary and not justifiable.

But it's hard to stay mad at Selma. Currently she has Alzheimer's. She's always asking the same questions over and over. She cannot recall the past. So how can I hold someone accountable for their actions when they no longer remember what those actions were and who they affected?

I recently visited Pops and found them watching TV together. Selma's eyes seemed like that of a child. Very innocent and barely absorbing the information presented to her. Pops showed me a vial of blood that he urinated, and this broke my heart. He explained that he had pancreatic cancer a second time (now at nearly eighty-five). He was able to have surgery, and they successfully removed the tumor, but this was a side effect.

I looked at them—so old now—and couldn't help but feel bad. They have no one but each other. Sure, they had grandchildren and children in the world, but on a day to day basis, have only each other for comfort.

I pray for their health and well-being and that God watches over them. Amen.

The interesting thing is that they are able to be in the same room together, alone. When I was growing up, they hated each other. Selma refused to be in the same room with Pops, and now she can't remember those things. I made sure to thank them for all they did for us and wished that they took care of themselves. I acknowledged the struggle they had and told them that I loved them. It felt good. Like a weight lifted from my chest.

POPS AND SELMA

Closure was the final leveler. It made one forget, move forward.

Pops began to cry and thanked me for visiting. I hugged him as I departed and asked him to call me should he ever need anything. I now acknowledge that they are my family. Whether or not by blood, they were there for me and raised me, and for that I am grateful.

39

SCANDY

It seems like fate brought Scandy and me together. Feels like just yesterday we met on the phone chat line, always an awkward detail to explain. So we'd start by explaining that we met for a hookup over the phone and that blossomed into true love eight years later. But before we got to all of the good stuff, there were definitely some challenges along the way.

A few months into our relationship, the typical issues of any relationship began to arise. We had conquered the HIV disclosure issue and moved on to building trust and an emotional bond. With each moment I could feel anxiety building around whether this was real or just another experience for the records. In fact after nine and a half years, I still find myself questioning that. But that is a whole other issue.

I remember falling in love with Scandy. It's funny because when I met him he was just a cute guy, not a partner. There was no knight, no special armor saying, I'm here, I'm the one. It never works out that way.

We worked together and stabilized Scandy's health to optimal, thank God, and just lived our lives. Scandy worked at Banana Republic, and I worked for Cosi. Every day we would meet up at the house or after work. We'd cuddle and talk and get to know each other. I'd tell him about my childhood and life experiences, and he'd just look at me with disbelief. He'd tell me of his experiences, like when his father died when he was ten, and how his mother raised him the best she could. How he didn't know he was poor as a child, something I was all too familiar with at a young age.

I remember one day we were having a deep conversation about my childhood, and he flat-out called me a liar. It was in reference to my dad and mom and the whole Russian roulette experience. After I told him the story, he said, "Get the fuck out of here. That's got to be bullshit. I'm sorry—I've listened to your stories and questioned some here and there, but this has got to be bullshit."

I replied, "It isn't, I swear . . . Well, maybe it is, because all of this time I've thought of it as a first memory, but it could have been a dream. Who knows? Maybe it was a dream, and I've interpreted it as a memory. But the details are so vivid, I think it was real."

During that discussion, we could hear the front door opening. Mom walked in, and we approached her. I said, "Yes! Mom, let me ask you a question because we were just talking about this, and Scandy doesn't believe me. Please tell me if I'm bugging out and had a dream or if this really happened. I remember, but it's faded, like a dream, Dad playing Russian roulette with you and pushing you into the bathroom and you hugging me and crying."

Mom cried, "Oh, my God, papi, you remember that?"

"Yeah, Mom, is it true?"

Mom was in tears. "I'm so sorry, papi. I didn't know you knew that! Yes, it is true—and how could you remember that! You were a baby."

"I don't know, that's what I've always thought of when I think of my first memory. Scandy made me question whether or not I was bugging out or it was a dream, but yeah."

Scandy looked at us in shock. "Wow, that's crazy. To be honest, I thought a lot of the stuff you've been telling me about your life was bullshit up until now. Damn ... Wow."

"Wow" is a familiar reaction to my life story. Too often I would share an experience here or there randomly with older folks, and they would almost always change their demeanor to that of empathy or sympathy. I never wanted for people to feel bad for me; I just shared deep shit in conversation. And even now there's the "wow." Or "I'm so sorry." Others have said I should write a book (joke's on them now) and seek counseling.

But the most enlightened responses have been from the few that said, "You know you said that, and it shocked me. I would never look at you and be able to tell that you've been through so much. You know that's not normal, right? That's some sad stuff, Eddie."

To those people I am grateful, because without their feedback, I would've still been walking this earth thinking that everything I had been through as a child was expected or " normal." That something I did or didn't do was the reason I went through what I did. Scandy is definitely a major contributor to how I process my past and present emotions. At one point I was a wreck. I still have moments. But it's the awareness that counts.

Honestly, when I met Scandy I was extremely insecure and had no trust for anybody outside of Mom, Kira, and the kids. After a few months, I began to worry about whether or not this guy was worth my time. I went through his cell phone and found call logs showing recent calls to the chat line. I became infuriated and demanded to know why he was still looking for hookups if I were to be his boyfriend.

I had no trust, and so many doubts! When he denied having bad intentions, I was convinced that he was just another dude who would fade eventually. I decided that I would stay with Scandy, but I would never be faithful to him. Be the player not the played.

I played Scandy every chance I got. I would clear my call logs, and do my dirt at cruising spots, all the while monitoring his logs and activities. (This was after I disclosed the HIV status, and he reciprocated.) It was also during the time I worked at my first job in the nonprofit sector. I was doing outreach to men who have sex with men, so it was very easy to find hookups. That job took me to Atlanta to the CDC where intervention strategies were being implemented and gave me venues where I could play while gaining professional experience. I even hooked up with a guy from the CDC. During one of the breakout sessions where we were brainstorming ideas for structural objectives, I flirted with him and he flirted back. We slipped away to "go to the bathroom" and he led me to an elevator that took us to the basement/pool area of the hotel. We proceeded to the bathroom and mutually masturbated and got off. We said nothing to one another and went back to the conference. This happened over and over for the next two days. He was hot and it was hot, but it was something that weighed heavily on my conscience, and I regretted it for some time.

When I got back to New York, I made it a point to work on our relationship. It's interesting how when you do dirt, you try to make up for it by being extra nice and focusing on what your partner is potentially doing wrong. Guilt. Conscience. Still I stuck to my motto, which was to be the player and not the played. One day after work I called Scandy and acted like I was on my way to another meeting but with the intention of surprising him to show up with flowers and dinner. Scandy said he was just playing video games and relaxing. We hung up, and I headed home. When I arrived I noticed that the TV was on and the lights were on, but nobody was home. I looked for Scandy in the closet and all and realized he wasn't home.

Instantly my suspicions arose, and I called him. No answer. Called again, then a few minutes after, I received a return call from Scandy, who said he was on his way back to the house— that he had just stepped out to smoke a blunt with his cousin Joanne really quickly. I knew he was lying, and when he came in, he had paranoia written all over his body. Scandy's not a good liar. He fidgets and his mouth dries up when he's lying. So after probing, I called his cousin and asked if he was with her.

"Tell Scandy I said to keep me out of his bullshit. I don't know what he was doing, but I am at work not at home, and I am not going to be lying for him." (I loved her for that.) She hung up.

We argued and hashed it out. I couldn't be mad. I had secrets, too. We spoke about the possibility of hooking up with guys together instead of cheating on each other. We agreed and began to chat online with guys for a potential hookup. And I consulted Mom. She approved. She felt that if we loved each other and didn't want to leave each other, we shouldn't have to and should work it out.

In retrospect, moving on with Scandy was definitely therapeutic and gave me a sense of what it was like to live a normal life. He and I began to enjoy the benefits of working two full-time positions, living alone, and being a regular couple. At work I was promoted to Case Manager for the Rikers Island program under the condition that I go to college. I signed up for college and began taking classes toward a business management degree. The change in position included a decent increase in pay. Scandy sought out new employment opportunities and became a manager for a health food chain in Midtown, which also included a decent pay increase. He even became the number one manager in his company.

After five years, there were challenges. We were both cheating! It came to light, and the relationship was at risk of ending. We fist fought, broke up, and somehow managed to come to an understanding. Somehow we worked it out, and things took a turn for the better. In this newfound way of interacting, we were able to express ourselves, and shared our innermost desires with each other.

After Mom passed, we spent three days telling each other stories of times we cheated. We gave each other scenarios, details, and reasons why we reacted in arguments the way we did. It was the most surreal, invigorating, scary, and exciting conversation. "You remember that time I said you were crazy, well you were actually spot on with your suspicions," Scandy said.

"Yeah, you never suspected, but remember that old friend of ours, well I was in love with him and about to leave you for him," I responded. The things we shared were incredible and surprisingly awkward.

We cried, laughed, got angry, and had lots of make-up sex. I wouldn't change how any of our relationship went for anything.

At this writing, we are no longer together as a couple, but that's another story for another time. We have been best friends for four years now. I forgive and forget all of those painful years of trying to make something that wasn't meant to be happen. There's so much that happened in the background throughout our relationship: lies, deceit, and what I thought was unforgivable madness. Perhaps one day I'll detail what happened and why we didn't work out. But for now all I will say is that I wish him the best and appreciate him for being a support to me and my family. He did the best he could given the circumstances—anyone else would've just run away.

Scandy will always have a special place in my heart and be a significant factor in my life, one that contributed to the man I am today. So for having loved me through the roughest experiences, he is appreciated. I love Scandy, always, unconditionally, and I look forward to continuing to learn more about him every day.

40

MOVING FORWARD

I have mentioned most of my family, but there are others who have gone unmentioned. So I take this time to acknowledge them. I have two sisters, Amanda and Nicole, who were from Helen through my dad. While I haven't spent a lot of time with them, the love and warmth that they've shown me when we do cross each other's paths is something of note. My sisters are all beautiful and unique in their personalities. Amanda recently began a nursing program, and she works two jobs aside from going to school full time. Like me, she's a go-getter. Nicole has recently given birth to a beautiful baby girl and is married, living her own life. I am very proud of them both and look forward to spending more time with them to catch up and be one another's support system.

I also have two brothers from Joanna and Marco, James

and Emmanuel. I don't really see them unless I stop by their home, but I make sure to do so every so often to check in and remind them that they are a part of my life.

My aunt Ella and I have had some really interesting follow-up conversations about past and present. She acknowledges that she was young, and her approaches toward a lot of the past transgressions were immature. For that, she has apologized. I can agree to disagree with her in how my behavior was, but she was a single parent of two who took the time and energy out of her difficult situation to obtain custody of us. A stressful and daunting process that I am all too familiar with. Every so often we text each other and check in. I feel bad for her because I understand what she was going through, and why even though she was so beautiful, she chose to be with men who abused her. She too was a victim of her genogram. A young woman who raised herself absent my grandmother and grandfather in the streets of New York City.

Speaking of my grandmother on my dad's side, I feel for her the most. She is diagnosed as paranoid schizophrenic, which is something that instills fear in my heart when thinking of my future. Her addictions to alcohol, marijuana, and cocaine drove her already existing mental illness to new heights. She now resides in a mental health nursing home where there are a lot of elderly mentally ill people who have no families and are basically waiting to die. I make it a point to visit her frequently to remind her that she has family and that I love her very much. I look forward to her eyes lighting up every time I go to visit her. She has limited cognitive function and semi-poor hygiene, but she remembers me and loves me, and that's all that matters. My dad makes sure to do her laundry and take her to do her hair from time to time. Her situation is a scary reality. She had several children and grandchildren yet she remains housed at a mental health shelter surrounded by madness. Will I grow old and wind up crazy? Will I too be alone? These questions always arise when visiting her. But I make sure to visit because if karma is real, then I think I'll be fine. I am paying my dues and investing energy into my family and friends so that if I ever do lose my mind or grow old, I won't be alone. Somebody has to remember me for being there and pay it forward—at least I hope so.

My ultimate goal was and continues to be to strike it big and become financially capable of removing my grandmother from there and to buy a huge house that my family can call home. The one thing that I can identify as a constant for all of us is the lack of a central home. A place where when all else fails, we know we can go to, to be around family and have support.

Kira and I are in a good place. I'd like to think that I am her first support above all others, something she has expressed to me and I love her dearly for. Marisa and I are also in a good place. She has been working for Prêt A Manger for almost three years now, and I am very proud of her for her growth and maturity. Robert and I see each other rarely, but I love him as much as I do all my siblings.

Sara is college bound and whom I consider my golden child. Don't get me wrong, I love them all the same, but I feel like Sara has benefited most from my influence. She has had ups and downs with me, but overall has always understood that I love her and want the best for all my siblings. She excelled in school and continues to remain in my care. We have a special bond. That kid is way beyond her time, a trait I can identify with.

As for Tamara, I fear for her. I love her so much and see so much damage that is almost beyond repair. She is self-destructive and has become desensitized to the point where she just lives day to day with no one to answer to. She lives this mystery life that no one is aware of. I hate that I have failed Tamara in not truly understanding that her actions were a result of her upbringing and being the youngest. I worry for her and hope that one of these days she changes her thought patterns. If she does, then I will gladly take the responsibility back on to support her in positive growth—and if not, I will love her unconditionally. I'll help her gain perspective.

There are many factors and details to consider when approaching my past and the kids. Sometimes it gives me a headache to try to process it all, but ultimately, I have come to the conclusion that what was done was done, and all that can be done about the past is making sure that each day at present is approached with optimism.

I can only try to create a new future rid of the curses of my genogram. I will try to be positive and create relationships that last and are meaningful. I will be forgiving and look at the past as not a factor leading to my doom but a road map from which to learn and to become a better man. I will use my experiences to see the pain and light in others and be supportive to anybody who faces abuse, struggle, addiction, and the realities of their genograms.

I forgive you Steve, Pops, Selma, Dad, Mom, and anyone else who wronged me. I pray that God gives you all the peace that I work toward obtaining every day. I also pray that my siblings all live meaningful, passionate, and successful lives free of oppression, addiction, and insanity. That they too find peace in this chaotic world and that they are afforded the opportunities I have been afforded so they can grow just as I have.

I will always be the voice of reason. The glue of the family! I used to feel like a punching bag, but now I accept my position as a family man. I love you all unconditionally, which is something Mom always emphasized as being key to any relationship. I promise that I will have faith, have honor, and try to be the man Mom always told me I would be. The way I think is a result of my experiences, but I have to move forward always, reminding myself that my reality is dictated by my thoughts, which make me who I am . If I want to go down in history as a good, genuine, and honorable person, I have to approach everything with optimism.

To be continued . . .Wish me luck!

I had come full circle. A man. Capable of making good decisions for myself. Of realizing I could not control everyone´s fate. That my powers were not limitless ...

I had been a father, a brother, a lover, a caregiver, a son, but I had ignored the most important role. Being me.

The mission became clear to me! To motivate and inspire anyone in my life path. To live my light and love from the heart in each moment. I will do my best. I love and accept myself - unconditionally...as you should yourself... and hopefully before we die.

Namaste!

If you enjoyed reading;

1. Please visit **EddiePabon.com** and contact me! I'd love to receive your feedback.

2. Follow me on social media! **@HaveHonorHaveFaith**

3. Post a picture with yourself, the book, and your review using the hashtag: **#TheSonWillRiseInDecember**

Thank you in advance for your support!